SHIPWRECK

THROW THAT S.H.I.T. OVERBOARD

CARMEN CALHOUN

MARIGOLD PRESS BOOKS

Published in Savannah, Georgia by Marigold Press Books.

Marigold Press Books titles may be purchased in bulk for educational, business, fundraising, or sales promotional use. For information, please email marigoldpressbooks@gmail.com.

Author: Calhoun, Carmen
Title: Shipwreck: Throw that S.H.I.T. Overboard
ISBN: 979-8-9985495-3-3 (softcover)
ISBN: 979-8-9985495-4-0 (eBook)
ISBN: 979-8-9985495-5-7 (Audio)
Library of Congress Control Number: 2025909491
Cover Design: Sadia Shahid
Illustrations: Jodi Caggige
Book Design: Russ Davis, Bravo Book Design

I lovingly dedicate this book to the memory of my late sister, Denise R. Wilkins; to Aretha Wills, Rodney Gross, and to all my siblings who shaped my story in ways both spoken and unspoken.

To my beloved nieces, Renita Gross and Jeanette Thornton, and to my greatest gifts—my children, Tiffany Solarin and Dwight Price—thank you for being my "Why."

And to my dear childhood friend, Marietta Johnson—thank you for being a light in the early chapters of my life, when joy was simple and friendship was everything. You are part of the root system that holds me steady.

ACKNOWLEDGEMENTS

There are far too many hands that held me, prayers that covered me, and hearts that believed in me to name them all—but I see you. I feel you. And I thank you.

A special thank you to Tammy Proctor, Alecia Prather, Rebekah McLeod, and Trish Brewer—for walking with me when I questioned the path, and for reminding me who I was when I forgot.

To Rebekah McLeod—thank you for your fierce, unwavering *tough love*. For every "no" you gave when I wanted a "yes," for every side-eye I threw and every standard you refused to lower—I'm grateful. You stood your ground, and this book is better for it.

They say great editors are worth their weight in gold. Rebekah and Morgan McLeod—you are gold. Pure, rare, and refining.

To the entire Marigold Press publishing family—thank you for your patience, your excellence, and for treating my story like it mattered. Because it did. Because it does.

And to my best friend, Adrienne Crews, who coached me through tears in that quiet hotel room—thank you. Your presence helped birth this book. I'll never forget that sacred space.

Author's Note

This is not just a book; it is an experience. *Shipwreck: Throw That S.H.I.T. Overboard* dives deep into Shame, Hurt, Insecurity, and Trouble with honesty, intensity, and heart. It is full of love, laughter, trauma, and awakening.

Trigger Warnings: Religious trauma, toxic family dynamics, manipulation, abandonment, emotional abuse, and grief around health decisions.

With Love and Fire,
Carmen Calhoun

CONTENTS

Shipwreck Playlist

A Soul Detox in Songs

1. "When God Says Move"—Carmen Calhoun
2. "This Animal"—Lauren McLeod Carter
3. "Dear Daughter"— Rebekah McLeod
4. "Safe"—Carmen Calhoun
5. "Free"—Lauren McLeod Carter
6. "He Loves"—Carmen Calhoun
7. "Rest"—Lauren McLeod Carter
8. "Sacred Romance"—Rebekah McLeod
9. "Worthy of It"—Rebekah McLeod
10. "The Invitation"—Carmen Calhoun
11. "Follow the Joy"—Rebekah McLeod
12. "Dare 2 Be U"—Carmen Calhoun
13. "Awesome God"—Carmen Calhoun
14. "I Am"—Carmen Calhoun

Scan the QR Code for Spotify Link

"Automatic rewind as the screen within my mind takes me back to the time when I was robbed without a gun and silenced out of fear. Can you tell me why this is happening? Can you tell me when it will end? Manually fast forward as I press toward my destiny, I take my thoughts captive and I forgive all those who have offended me, including me, and I tell myself I am NOT my past, I am . . . The head and not the tail, I am above and not beneath, I am strong, I am rich, I am healed. I am His." —Carmen Calhoun

Introduction
THE VISION BEHIND THE VOYAGE

My childhood story, woven with threads of laughter, whispered secrets, and tears, holds a peculiar yet fondly remembered setting: our family's single, modestly sized bathroom. This cramped 5x8 space was a universe of its own, rich with stories and moments that shaped my early years.

The bathroom, with its door narrowly avoiding a collision with the toilet, and a small sink capped by a mirrored medicine cabinet, was the stage for many of life's dramas and comedies. The bathtub under the window, more than just fixtures, witnessed the covert meetings of my nieces, my sister, and sometimes my nephews. But mostly it was my nieces and me who turned this tiny room into our secret council chamber and, many times, an escape room from my short-tempered mother. If you ever needed to disappear, the bathroom was your best bet—until someone banged on the door demanding justice (or just their turn).

Privacy? What a joke. In our bustling household, the concept of alone time was about as real as a unicorn in the backyard. Our bathroom rendezvous were thrilling, not just for the secrets we shared, but for the sheer chaos of trying to squeeze in our confessions before someone else barged in. It was here, amidst steam, the occasional mystery puddle, and echoes of laughter, that we dared to dream aloud and share our deepest secrets.

Our gatherings often featured an improvised ballet between my nieces and me: one of us using the toilet, while another perched on the edge of the tub, and another sat Indian-style on the floor, squeezed between the tub and the toilet like we were in some kind of survivalist training camp. We had an unspoken rule: acknowledge nothing, smell nothing, and brace yourself for whatever chaos unfolded next. Questions were not just asked; they were interrogations—rapid-fire, relentless, and often completely ridiculous. Survival in that bathroom meant sacrificing personal space, turning a blind eye (and nose), and accepting that dignity was a luxury we simply couldn't afford. But those moments, ridiculous and real, became cherished memories of solidarity and sisterhood.

Amidst these tender recollections, one incident stands out, bridging the gap between humor and the absurd. On a day like any other while taking a bath, my older sister, armed with a deodorant can and a mischievous glint in her eye, decided my most private area was in dire need of "freshening up." Before I could process what the hell was happening, a cold, stinging blast hit me like an arctic wind. I let out a shriek so high-pitched that dogs three blocks away probably perked up, the icy burn searing both my skin and my trust in humanity.

Enter parental justice—fast, furious, and punctuated by the kind of good old-fashioned ass-whooping that was practically a household tradition back in the day, ensuring my sister thought twice before attempting another bathroom ambush. Her prank, meant to be funny, quickly turned into one of those "well, that escalated quickly" moments. But time has a way of turning trauma into comedy, and now, instead of horror, it's a tale we revisit with wheezing laughter and exaggerated reenactments. The bathroom was a haven and a battleground, a space where privacy was a joke, but bonds were unshakable. Lessons in boundaries, respect, and, apparently, the dangers of unsupervised deodorant, were all learned in that cramped little room.

Reflecting on these moments, I'm struck by how such a small, overused bathroom could hold so much drama, sisterhood, and straight-up foolishness. It was the site of one of my earliest lessons in the unexpected ways people can hurt you. Even if I had learned to laugh off the surface wounds, I still hadn't figured out what to do with the ones that sank deeper.

People go to the bathroom for the usual reasons—handling their business, scrubbing off the day, or hiding from responsibilities for an extra five minutes. But beyond the basics, the bathroom is also an unsung hero—a place where walls come down, both figuratively and literally. It's where deep thoughts creep in uninvited, where tears mix with steam, and where existential crises hit hardest. It's the one room where you can lock the door and pretend the outside world doesn't exist, even if it's just for a few stolen moments. The bathroom isn't just a pit stop—it's a confessional, a war room, and a sanctuary all rolled into one.

I had a dream once where I was in an enormous, beautifully designed bathroom with the most stunning fixtures. A girlfriend of mine stood beside me at the sink, applying makeup—at least, that's what I assumed. I was seated on the toilet, and the scene felt normal at first, casual even.

Then, I reached for toilet tissue—nothing. The roll was empty. Panic set in. I began to yell, "I need some toilet tissue!" As I looked up, my eyes landed on the open bathroom door, and I was astonished—not just because it was open, but because it was positioned directly in front of the most dynamic, eye-catching shower I had ever seen. The contrast between its beauty and my predicament made the moment even more surreal.

And then, out of nowhere, toilet tissue appeared—unraveling from the doorway in a long, winding trail straight to me. But relief turned to horror the moment I saw it. The tissue wasn't clean. It was smeared with feces, tangled, and somehow grotesquely attached to me. It clung like an accusation, an unavoidable, humiliating mess that now felt like a part of me.

In an instant, the pristine elegance of the bathroom meant nothing. The gleaming fixtures, the breathtaking shower—all of it was overshadowed by the undeniable, stomach-churning reality of what was happening. The filth wasn't just there—it had found me, claimed me. And no matter how desperately I wanted to shake it off, it stuck, an unwelcome truth I couldn't escape.

I kept saying, "Ew, ew, ew, that's nasty!" while yelling again for more toilet tissue—even as I kept reusing the same filthy piece. The realization hit me like a slap. I was disgusted, horrified, asking myself, "Why did I do that?"

I woke up immediately, my heart pounding, and asked Daddy (God), "What does this mean?"

His response was as blunt as it was shocking: *You have a trail of S.H.I.T. following behind you that you don't smell anymore, but it stinks.*

I was floored, completely floored. Did You just say 'shit'?! I kept asking Him, as if my ears had betrayed me. But Daddy was unfazed.

Carmen, get past Me saying that word and hear what I said. You give power to that word as derogatory, not Me. Do what you always do.

Hmmm. That last part—"Do what you always do"—hit me. I knew exactly what He meant: Look it up.

So, I did. I called a few of my girlfriends first, needing to process this moment, but also craving validation. Some were in awe, some laughed, and others weren't sure whether to believe me or not. But that didn't stop me.

I typed into Google: "What is the origin of the word shit?"

The first thing I saw claimed it was an urban legend. But the Holy Spirit nudged me. *Read on.*

And so, I did.

Back in the day, certain types of manure were transported by ship—because, well, everything was transported by ship back then. In its dry form, manure was much lighter, easy to store, and seemingly harmless. But the moment water seeped in, the game changed. Fermentation kicked in, methane gas built up, and with a single lantern or stray spark—BOOM. Entire ships went up in flames before anyone realized what was happening.

After too many explosive lessons learned the hard way, sailors began marking ships carrying manure bundles with the letters S.H.I.T.—short for "Ship High In Transit." The idea was simple: Keep it stored high above the lower decks, far from any water, to prevent another floating disaster.

I sat with this, running my fingers across the words on the screen, and I heard Daddy say: *You're the ship.*

I blinked. "Hmmm." That was all I had. But the longer I sat with it, the more it gnawed at me.

Finally, I asked, "Okay, but what am I carrying that's so dangerous?"

And Daddy, without missing a beat, answered: *Shame, Hurt, Insecurity, and Troubles. S.H.I.T.*

I exhaled, letting the weight of that truth settle. Wow. I hadn't seen it before, but now it was glaring.

Daddy didn't just drop that word to shock me. He was leading me somewhere. The weight I had been carrying, fermenting in the dark, was about to explode. And when I looked at it for what it was—Shame, Hurt, Insecurity, Troubles—it hit me like a wrecking ball.

Then came the kicker: *Jesus paid it all. It's not by your works. You are no longer in the bosom of your parents—you are seated with Christ in high places. Get rid of it.*

The words cut through me like a blade—sharp, undeniable, and full of truth. Here I was, carrying around all this emotional baggage, keeping it tucked in the lower decks of my soul where it festered, turned toxic, and threatened to take me down. I had been holding on to things that had no place in my future, things that had already been accounted for, already paid in full. I had to make a choice. Either I could keep carrying the weight of my past—letting it sabotage my peace, my body, and my life—or I could throw that S.H.I.T. overboard and sail higher.

After this dream of symbolic discovery, I found myself in a no-nonsense conversation with the Divine—not in some booming voice from the heavens, but in the quiet, surreal aftermath of a dream about searching for toilet paper in a metaphorical bathroom. Because of course, even divine revelations come wrapped in absurdity. This quest wasn't just about wiping away the surface mess—it was a deep dive into the S.H.I.T. I had been carrying for way too long, dead weight that had me stuck reliving an unexamined past.

The Divine, with a wild sense of humor, hit me with an urban legend about transporting manure by sea—how if it got wet, it could ferment and explode. And just like that, I got the message: my internal baggage, left unchecked, was a ticking time bomb. The same S.H.I.T. that could be used to fertilize growth was also the same S.H.I.T. that could blow my life to hell, if I didn't manage it right.

Then came the next level of truth: the soiled toilet tissue in my dream. It wasn't just about past mistakes—it was about the recycled negativity, the cycles of self-sabotage that kept leaving fresh stains on my soul. The Divine was schooling me in some real-life waste management: stop carrying what's meant to be flushed.

And then there was my sister-girl Adrienne, who once hit me with a side-eye so sharp it could cut glass and said, "Carmen, your soul doesn't trust you."

Excuse me?

I laughed it off at first, but she wasn't playing. When I asked what she meant, she doubled down: "You just keep lying to yourself."

Whew. That one stung.

And after months—hell, years—of dodging the truth, it finally smacked me like a brick to the face. I was out of alignment. Not slightly off course—nah, I was full-on, GPS-recalculating, making a U-turn immediately, lost. I would say I wanted one thing but do the complete opposite. I had mastered the art of self-betrayal, and the receipts were all over my life. My discipline was trash. And discipline? That's the highest form of self-love.

But here's the thing—I didn't need to force myself into discipline like I was in some military boot camp for the soul. What I needed was a shift in thinking. Because when you change your mind about something, you don't have to strong-arm yourself into action—you just flow in alignment with what you believe. If I stopped treating consistency like a punishment and started seeing it as freedom, I wouldn't keep wrecking my progress every time I got bored or in my feelings.

The truth? My inconsistency wasn't about laziness. It was about unhealed wounds. Wounds that made me second-guess my own worth. Wounds that tricked me into believing that if things were going too well, I'd eventually mess it up anyway—so why even try? Wounds that resisted discipline because chaos had become my comfort zone.

But discipline—real, healthy discipline—isn't about restriction. It's not about proving anything. It's about protecting what's sacred. It's about creating a life where my soul could finally exhale because it knew I wasn't about to abandon myself again. As if abandoning myself could cause me to be alone.

And listen—you are not that powerful. You don't have the ability to be truly alone. I know how easy it is to feel like you're out here raw-dogging life with no backup, but that's a lie. And not even a creative one. That's just Shame talking, trying to convince you that isolation is protection when really, it's just another trap.

I used to believe I had no one. That when it came down to it, I was the only person I could count on. I had my plans, my strategies, my "I'll just figure it out" mentality—and Lord, did I wear that independence like a badge of honor.

But that badge? Heavy as hell.

I carried it like a weight strapped to my chest, convinced that if I didn't do it all myself, it wouldn't get done. And the worst part? I thought I was alone by necessity, not by choice. That the support I longed for didn't exist.

Until one day, I was sitting in my car, stressed beyond belief, drowning in my own thoughts when I felt it—not a voice, not words, just a presence. It was as if something whispered straight into my spirit:

You are not alone. You have never been alone. You just stopped listening.

And whew, that hit different. Because in that moment, I realized the truth: I had spent so much time tuning into the fear-based nonsense in my head that I had tuned out the very presence of God within me. I had ignored the Holy Spirit—the One who had been guiding me all along, nudging me, covering me, surrounding me.

I wasn't alone. I had never been alone. I had just let my wounds convince me otherwise.

But the Holy Spirit? Different energy entirely. The Holy Spirit reminds you of your *Beloved Identity*—that you are seen, held, known. That you are surrounded, even when you don't feel it. That love is not something you have to earn—it's something that has been chasing you down all along.

And when you realize that? When you actually *believe* that?

You move differently. You stop trying to muscle through life like you're the only one in the fight. You stop mistaking isolation for strength. You start making decisions that reflect the truth:

You are loved. You are covered. You are never truly alone.

And that? That changes everything.

The Divine, whom I affectionately call "Daddy," didn't just hand me a revelation on a silver platter—nah, He dragged me through a whole process of gut-checks and truth bombs. He showed me that if I really wanted to clean up my S.H.I.T., I had to stop treating it like a souvenir. Love, compassion, forgiveness, and gratitude weren't just feel-good buzzwords; they were the scrub brushes I needed to scrape off the layers of self-inflicted grime.

But let's be real—this wasn't some magical, overnight transformation. This path required some real-deal courage, the kind that makes you ugly cry in the mirror. It meant self-reflection so raw it burned, and a commitment to transformation that felt like detoxing from a lifetime of bad habits. It was a slow, messy process of unlearning and relearning; but at the other end of it? Joy, peace, and fulfillment that didn't feel like some distant dream—a reality I was finally making room for.

Truth be told, it wasn't always slow. Some shifts happened in an instant, the moment I stopped wrestling and simply aligned with the truth of who God said I am. Some burdens fell off like dead weight the second I stopped arguing with grace and simply received it. Other lessons, though? Those were stubborn, dragging me through round after round of resistance before I finally surrendered. Healing wasn't always a gentle unfolding; sometimes it was a full-on demolition, breaking down the lies I had built my identity on so I could finally stand in something real.

The vision behind this book is one of liberation and healing, not just for me, but for anyone who dares to embark on this journey. I want to provide a beacon for those navigating through the stormy seas of life, searching for a lighthouse to guide them home. Through the pages of this book, you are invited to confront your own shipwrecks, discover the pearls of wisdom that lie in facing your deepest fears, and learn that forgiveness—of others and yourself—is the wind that fills the sails of your soul, propelling you towards new horizons.

As you turn these pages, may you find the courage to throw overboard the weights that anchor you to the past, allowing your spirit to soar into the boundless skies of possibility.

Welcome to the voyage of a lifetime, a journey not just of reading, but of profound transformation. Welcome aboard *"Shipwreck: Throw that S.H.I.T. Overboard."*

Let the voyage begin!

Chapter One

STRANDED BY SHAME

Shame is that unrelenting, sneaky little bastard that slithers into your mind and convinces you that one mistake defines your entire existence. It's like your inner critic took steroids and grabbed a megaphone. Shame doesn't need an audience—it thrives in the lonely corners of your mind, whispering nonsense like, "You ain't shit, and you never will be." And the worst part? It doesn't just stay in your head. Oh no, it seeps into your body—tight shoulders, shallow breath, stomach in knots. In his book, "When the Body Says No: Exploring the Stress-Disease Connection," Dr. Gabor Maté teaches that trauma and Shame don't just live in memory, they *live in the body*, shaping how we carry ourselves, react to situations, and even how we breathe.[1]

Shame is the emotional equivalent of an auntie who shows up at every family gathering, unbothered and uninvited, with unsolicited opinions and a mystery casserole nobody asked for.

As humans, we need to belong. It's wired into us. We stick with our people, our crew, our folks, because deep down, we know our survival depends on it. But when your own family is the first to make you feel like an outsider, that need for acceptance turns into a full-blown insecurity crisis with a side of "maybe I really was a factory defect."

My siblings made sure I got the message loud and clear. According to them, I *was* a mistake, a factory recall, an unfortunate

1 Gabor Maté, *When the Body Says No: Exploring the Stress-Disease Connection* (Hoboken: John Wiley & Sons Inc., 2011).

oops that somehow slipped through the cracks. And just to drive it home, they swore up and down that I was born in a toilet. (Which, for the record, I was NOT.) When I finally got fed up and ran to my mother for backup, thinking she'd at least pretend to be outraged, she hit me with, "All of you were mistakes." *Oh. Well then. So much for maternal reassurance.* I guess she thought she was being fair, making sure none of us felt special in our unplanned existence, but all I heard was, *Yep, you weren't supposed to be here.*

That feeling of not belonging wasn't just in my head—it followed me everywhere. Like the time I went to my grandmother's house, thinking I'd get to hang out with my nieces and my Aunt M, who were playing cards. I barely made it to the back door before my aunt popped up, and before I could say a word, SLAP. No warning, no explanation, just a good old-fashioned "sit your ass down somewhere" kind of smack. My ears were still ringing when they started laughing, telling me to get lost because I wasn't welcome. And that's when it clicked—I wasn't just an outsider in the family, I was the uninvited guest who kept showing up hoping for a seat at a table that was never set for me.

I ran home, back under the old English walnut tree that separated my grandmother's house from ours. My face was still stinging, but the slap wasn't what hurt most—it was the rejection. I ran straight to my father, thinking surely he would step in, handle this, make it right. His response? "Don't go over there anymore." That's it. That was his grand solution. No defense, no outrage, no "Who the hell do they think they are putting hands on my child?" Just a verbal shrug and a dismissal. His silence hit harder than the slap. It was like he was saying, *You're on your own, kid.*

And in my little kid mind, that silence wasn't just about my aunt—it was about me. It was confirmation that I wasn't worth standing up for. That's the thing about Shame. It doesn't always kick down the door screaming—it sneaks in through the cracks, settles into the spaces where love should be but isn't. Sometimes, Shame is just the absence of protection, the lack of affirmation, the hollow space where security should be, but damn sure ain't. My father's silence didn't just teach me to stay away from my grandmother's house; it taught me I wasn't worth fighting for. And that seed? Oh, it got planted deep—watered by every rejection, fed by every dismissal, growing into a thick, tangled root system of *I ain't enough* that took years to dig out.

Shame had settled into my bones before I even knew what to call it. Trauma doesn't just live in the mind—it gets stored in the body. It sinks into your stomach, makes your shoulders ache like you're carrying a weight you don't even realize is there.

My body had memorized rejection before my brain even caught up.

So what did I do? I laughed and sang through it. Made jokes and songs out of it. Shrugged it off like it didn't sting. Because if I could turn pain into comedy or a song, maybe—just maybe—it wouldn't hurt so much. But here's the thing about that kind of coping: it doesn't heal a damn thing. It just teaches you how to carry the wounds without breaking—until one day, you realize you're tired of carrying that shit at all.

There were two voices in my head: one was the get-up-and-go hustler, the one that pushed me to be better, to grind, to make something out of myself. That voice had me out there proving people wrong before they even had the chance to doubt me. But then there was the other one—the dysfunctional critic—the one that didn't want me to rise, the one whispering, *Stay small, don't get too loud, don't think you're special, 'cause the world will snatch you back down real quick.* And the worst part? That critic thought she was doing me a favor.

One of the clearest memories of that critic came straight from my daddy's mouth: "Sugar babe, you use your head for a hat rack." Now, maybe he thought he was being funny, maybe he thought he was dropping some old-school wisdom—who knows? But to me? That phrase hit like a gut-punch I could never forget. It played on repeat in my head like a scratched-up record stuck on the worst part of the song. And when you hear something enough times, it stops sounding like an opinion—it starts sounding like *truth.*

And let's be real—when the people who are supposed to uplift you are the same ones feeding your doubts, you start second-guessing every little thing about yourself. That critic didn't just live in my head—it lived in my bones, in my breath, in the way I second-guessed my own brilliance before I even let it shine.

Shame even made its way into my mothering. For instance, I remember an incident with my daughter, who loves interpreting art, particularly art on cards like tarot and oracle decks. In a moment of pure frustration and ignorance, I snapped, tore into her passion because I had boxed God into an ancient text-only view, and I made her cry. The truth is, God loves her and is captivated and astonished by her visual awareness. Who was I to call it witchcraft just because we had different lived experiences? That was the moment Papa asked me, "What's more important— your opinion…your right to be right…or the relationship?" I had to swallow that rock-hard pill of truth and choose the relationship.

In fact, she read me with her cards and was SPOT ON! She kept saying "Shundala!" So I asked her what exactly that meant, and she said, "Ma, y'all told me that if I didn't speak in tongues, I was going to hell." I immediately told her, "I never told you that," and she replied, "Other family members did."

She told me how she had been in the bathroom, crying out to God, hands raised, Black Gospel music blaring, full-on weeping—begging God to give her the Spirit language. And all she got was "Shundala." She said, "That's all you got for me, Lord? Just Shundala?!" And then she heard the Lord reply, *You are going to change the world with that one word!*

She said, "I receive it, Lord. Shundala."

Afterward, I realized the hurt I caused and began to feel guilt and shame, focusing solely on my perceived failure as a mother. At that moment, I wasn't even thinking about the impact on her—I was too busy beating myself up, replaying my words like a crime scene investigation. That's the trap of Shame: It locks you in self-condemnation so tightly that you can't even see the person you hurt, let alone heal the wound.

When you examine Shame down to its core, it's not simply a collection of uncomfortable feelings—it's a full-scale assault on your identity. Shame isn't content with making you feel bad about what you've done; it goes straight for the jugular, convincing you that *what you've done is who you are*. At its core, Shame is the puppeteer, pulling the strings of Guilt, Avoidance, Loneliness, and Regret, ensuring that your self-worth stays bound and gagged in the corner.

The Molecular Structure of Shame

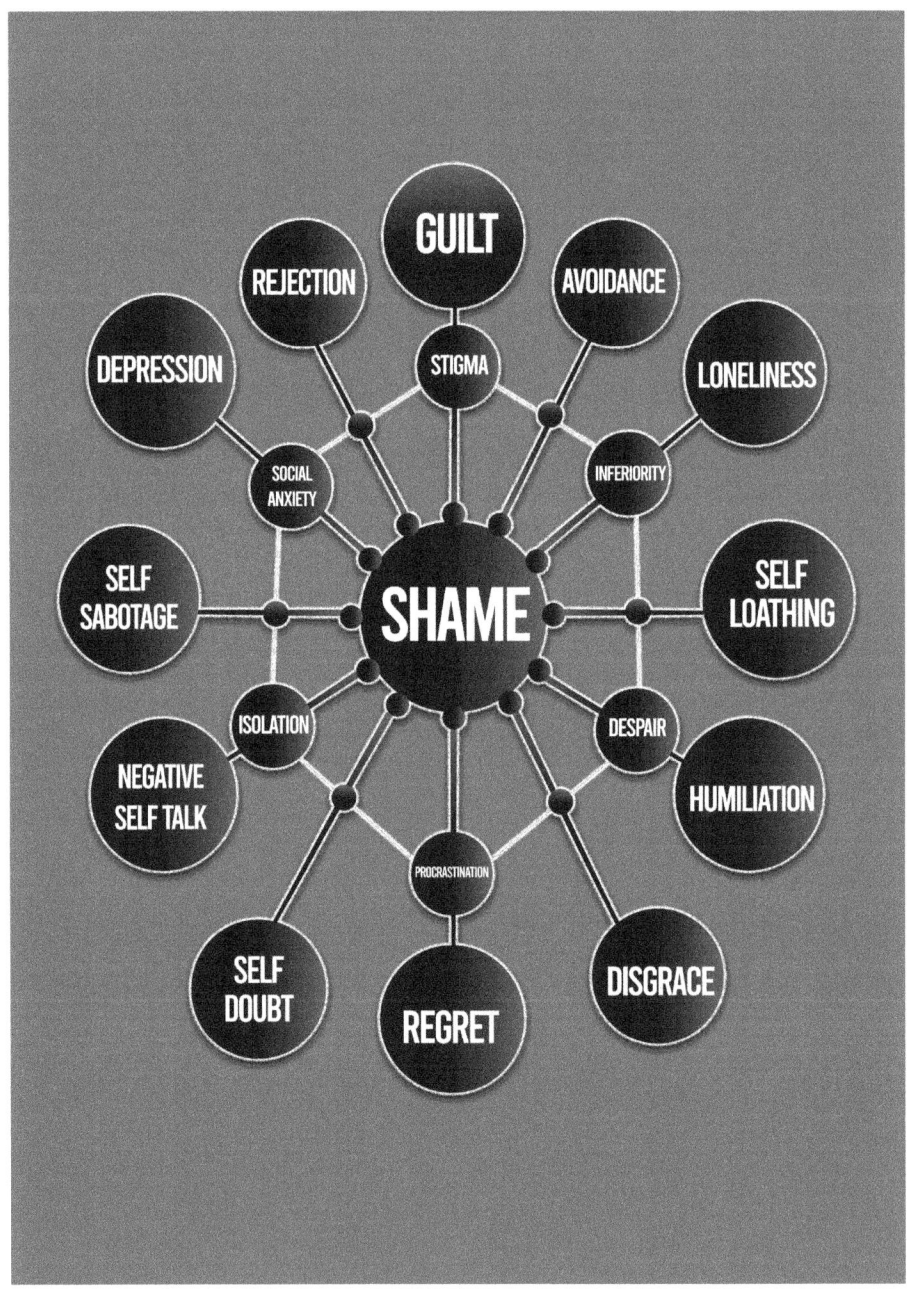

Image created by Sadia Shahid

The interconnectedness of Shame's molecular structure reveals how quickly it can take root. A single experience of Guilt can spiral into Self-Loathing, dragging Loneliness and Emotional Numbness along for the ride. Shame is a master manipulator, taking every mistake, every misstep, and turning it into a permanent marker on the whiteboard of your life.

One of the most vivid stories of Shame for me was that moment when my aunt's slap echoed not just through the room but through my entire sense of self. The real wound wasn't on my cheek—it was on my soul. Additionally, the silence of my father became the first brick in a wall of Shame that would take decades to dismantle.

Shame manifested as Guilt, convincing me that I deserved the slap, that my worth was as fragile as the silence that followed. It evolved into Avoidance, a need to hide, to remain unseen, hoping that if I stayed small enough, Shame wouldn't find me again. But of course, Shame knows every hiding spot. It seeped into my relationships, creating barriers of Loneliness and a crippling fear of vulnerability.

In my bathroom vision, the soiled toilet paper dragging behind wasn't just an embarrassing image—it was a tapestry of Shame. Each square represented a moment when Shame rewrote the narrative, turning moments of hurt into lifelong stories of inadequacy. Shame had become the editor of my life, cutting out joy and pasting in doubt.

But in that vision, the power of the Divine showed up. It was the revelation that Shame only had the power I gave it. As I entered into my own healing practices, including Breathwork (which I will talk more about in the Practices section) the narrative shifted from "I am not enough" to "I am loved, I am whole, I am seen." The tangled mess of Shame began to unravel, each exhale releasing another strand of the story.

The "Friends" in Our Head

For over 40 years, my best friend Renah and I had some of the realest, most unfiltered conversations about life. And one thing she always said was, *"The friends in my head told me…"* She treated those voices like they were on payroll—fully convinced they were speaking nothing but facts. And to top it off, she had this philosophy she swore by: *"If it doesn't make sense, it's a lie."* That was her whole gospel. If something didn't fit her logic, she shut it down on sight.

Now, you already know we butted heads over this. I'd tell her, *"Just because you don't understand something doesn't mean it's a lie—it just means you don't understand it."* But her "friends" weren't trying to hear that. They dug their heels in, confident as ever, arguing their case like they had a law degree.

And this wasn't just some harmless difference of opinion. This was about how these inner critics—the so-called "friends" in our heads—shape what we believe. These voices don't just pop up out of nowhere. They're built from our past, our fears, our wounds. And once they get comfortable? Whew, they'll run the whole damn show.

Renah's "friends" were some strong-willed debaters. To them, the world was black and white—either it made sense, or it wasn't real. But the problem is, these inner voices don't always tell the truth. They tell *their* truth, which is usually twisted by insecurity, pain, or just straight-up misinformation. And that's what our inner critics do. They don't come with receipts or proof—but they sure do *sound* confident.

Our inner critics are messy. They don't just mess with our own heads, they have us looking at other people sideways too. If you already think you're not good enough, these voices will convince you that everybody else thinks so too. If something doesn't make sense to you, they will swear up and down that it's wrong for *everyone*. They project our fears onto the world, distorting our reality and how we see the people around us.

See, the critics we carry are powerful. That functional critic? It made me tough, gave me drive, made sure I never backed down from a challenge. It pushed me past limits and helped me rise. But here's the catch—what once kept me going was no longer serving me. That hypervigilant, prove-everybody-wrong energy? It was exhausting. I didn't need to fight battles I had already won. I didn't need to prove my worth—I was born worthy.

My worth was never up for negotiation. It wasn't something I had to earn through accomplishments, perfection, or meeting someone else's standards. I didn't arrive on this planet with a checkbox of requirements to fill before I could call myself enough. No, my worth was woven into my being the moment I drew my first breath. My worth wasn't contingent on my productivity, my appearance, or my ability to fit into someone else's mold. Worthiness was my birthright, not a title I had to hustle for.

I didn't need to keep carrying the weight of someone else's silence. That burden? It wasn't mine to hold anymore. I was done dragging around the baggage of other people's unspoken words, unmet expectations, and unresolved pain. When I recognized the outdated thought processes, I released it all and stood in the truth of who I am—already chosen, already loved, already whole. The freedom of this truth is my inheritance, and I intend to fully own it, unapologetically and with an open heart.

And that dysfunctional critic? It had overstayed its welcome. That voice—the one that held me back, convinced me that no matter what I achieved, I still wasn't enough—it was time for that one to go. I didn't need to carry that fear anymore. I didn't need to let Doubt and Shame ride shotgun in my life. And I sure as hell didn't need my daddy's words playing on repeat in my head like some broken record: *Sugar babe, you use your head for a hat rack.* Nah. That track was getting deleted from the playlist.

Because the real failure? It wasn't in being bold. It wasn't in going too far, in standing out, in taking up space. The real failure was letting Shame win. Letting it keep me small. Letting it make me *believe* I didn't deserve more. And I do.

That's why I love that moment in Genesis 3:11 (NIV) when God asks Adam: *"Who told you that you were naked?"* That wasn't just about sin—it was about perception. Adam and Eve had always been naked, but they didn't feel Shame about it until they listened to the wrong voice. And that's the exact same way our inner critics work. *Who told you that?* Who told you you're not smart enough? Who told you you're not worthy? Who told you that just because you don't understand something, it can't be real?

These voices—whether they come from childhood wounds, society's expectations, or our own fears—need to be checked. Renah's favorite line, *"If it doesn't make sense, it's a lie,"* wasn't entirely wrong. But the real lie isn't always in what doesn't make sense—it's in what keeps us from growing, from seeing truth beyond our own experiences.

When we start questioning these voices, they lose their grip. They no longer get to dictate our worth, our abilities, or how we see the world. We stop letting doubt and fear shape our reality. We stop looking at others through the lens of our own insecurities. And we start trusting ourselves more, realizing that just because something doesn't fit into our current understanding doesn't mean it's not valuable, real, or true.

See, the "friends" in my head weren't actually friends. They were the voices of fear—voices that echoed old hurts, past betrayals, and generational wounds. They sounded familiar, which made them *feel* true, but they weren't. And here's where discipline comes in—because discipline is what helps you discern the difference between fear's voice and God's voice. The *friends in your head* will have you out here questioning your worth, expecting rejection, and anticipating failure before you even start. They will have you believing that isolation is protection when really, it's a prison.

So next time the "friends" in your head start talking recklessly, ask yourself one simple question: *Who told me that?* Because if that voice isn't lifting you up, it sure as hell doesn't deserve the mic.

Beloved Identity: The Antidote to Shame

Here's the truth: Shame doesn't get the final word. Sometimes, it's the very pressure that reveals the diamond within. Just like gold is refined through fire, Shame can be the catalyst that pushes you to strip away lies and step into the truth of your Beloved Identity.

Beloved Identity is the deep, unshakable understanding that your worth is not defined by your actions, achievements, or failures but by the eternal truth that you are deeply loved by God. It is the state of being fully known, fully seen, and fully loved—without condition. This love is not transactional; it remains constant, unwavering, and grounded in the truth that nothing can separate you from the love of God.

Dr. Gabor Maté, an expert on trauma and childhood development, teaches that Shame is not merely a fleeting feeling of guilt but a deep-rooted sense of unworthiness.[2] It often stems from unmet childhood needs, trauma, and the internalized belief that "I am not enough." According to Dr. Maté, when our authentic self is not accepted, we adapt by creating a version of ourselves that we believe will secure love and safety. This adaptation disconnects us from our true selves, creating fertile ground for Shame.

While Shame thrives in the shadows of "not enough," creating a narrative of constant striving for validation, Beloved Identity offers a powerful counter to this dynamic. It speaks to the wounded inner child, affirming that you are loved, accepted, and valued simply because you exist. It eliminates the need to perform, adapt, or earn approval, providing unconditional love that bypasses merit and anchors you in the inherent truth of your worth.

From Dr. Maté's perspective, healing involves reconnecting with your authentic self—the part of you that has always been worthy of love but was hidden beneath layers of adaptation and Shame. Beloved Identity creates a safe internal space where your authentic self can re-emerge, free from the need to hide or contort to fit external expectations. It is a return to your true self, where Shame loses its power, and love becomes the lens through which you see yourself and the world.

Beloved Identity shifts the perspective from striving to receiving. Instead of believing, "I am a failure," you begin to hear, "I am loved, even when I fail." Mistakes transform from evidence of unworthiness into opportunities for grace and growth. You no longer seek approval because you are already standing in Divine Approval. Your worth is not up for negotiation—you are already chosen, already seen, already held in love.

---

2 *The Wisdom of Trauma,* directed by Maurizio Benazzo and Zaya Benazzo. (2021; San Francisco, CA: The Hive Studios), Kinema.

Ways Beloved Identity Helps You Overcome Shame

1. *Nurturing the Inner Child and Restoring Authenticity:*
   Beloved Identity offers the love, acceptance, and
   validation that may have been missing in early life. By
   reparenting your inner child, you create a safe space
   to express your true feelings and experiences, breaking
   the cycle of shame that thrives in secrecy and silence.
   This nurturing approach helps restore connection to
   your authentic self, allowing you to show up without
   fear of being unworthy or unlovable.

2. *Breaking Self-Abandonment and Embracing
   Vulnerability:* Instead of abandoning your needs to
   maintain attachment with others, Beloved Identity
   calls you back to yourself. It strengthens your courage
   to be open about your struggles and fears, knowing
   that your identity is secure. This openness not only
   reduces the grip of Shame but also fosters deeper
   connections with others.

3. *Creating Safe Spaces for Self-Compassion:* Beloved
   Identity teaches you to view yourself through a lens
   of grace and understanding. By offering compassion
   to your wounded parts, you disrupt the cycle of self-
   condemnation and create an internal environment
   where you can heal and thrive.

4. *Releasing Shame and Walking in Freedom*: When you
   see yourself through the lens of divine love, you
   understand that you are not defined by your past or
   wounds. This perspective is redemptive and healing,

allowing you to walk confidently into the light and move freely without fear of being less loved, regardless of what you uncover about yourself.

5. *Extending Forgiveness and Breaking Cycles of Condemnation*: Unconditional love empowers you to forgive yourself and others. It shifts your focus from judgment to grace, enabling you to break free from cycles of Shame and condemnation and create a life rooted in freedom and wholeness.

Practical Tools for Releasing Shame

Breathwork: Try a technique called box breathing: inhale for 4 seconds; hold the inhale at the top for 4 seconds; exhale slowly for 4 seconds; hold the exhale at the bottom for 4 seconds. Each breath is a reminder that you are not your past—you are your potential.

Journaling: What is your first memory of Shame? How did it shape your self-perception?

Affirmations: Stand in front of the mirror and declare: "I am not what happened to me. I am not my mistakes. I am whole, I am loved, I am enough."

Community: Surround yourself with voices that speak truth, drowning out the whispers of Shame.

Visualization: Close your eyes and imagine carrying a cargo box marked "Shame" and throwing it overboard. What does it feel like to let it go?

Music for Meditation

"Worthy of it"
by Rebekah McLeod, feat. Carmen Calhoun

Chapter Two

IN THE HEADWINDS OF HURT

Hurt isn't only what happens to us—it's the meaning we assign to those experiences. It's the twisted little stories we tell ourselves, the ones that say, "This happened because I wasn't enough. Because I didn't matter." Sadhguru suggests that whenever someone or something hurts you, you can become either wise or wounded.[3] Most of us don't choose wisdom right away. We wallow, ruminate, and sometimes let that pain fester until it becomes part of our identity. But pain is supposed to be a teacher, not a permanent resident.

As children, my sister and I would lie on our parents' bed for hours, talking and laughing with our dad. That was our little safe haven, where everything felt light and easy. Now, my mom? She was a whole character—loved to gossip, always kept some drama brewing. But one thing about her? She could throw down in the kitchen. No matter what chaos was swirling, nobody in that house or neighborhood ever went hungry.

The energy in our home was like a seesaw—peaceful one minute, tense the next. Even though my mom stirred up trouble with her endless gossip, she had a big heart for taking care of people, and food was her love language. The air would shift when my dad, in his calm but firm way, checked her when she got too deep in the mess. And just like that, the balance would reset. Back to peace. Back to laughter. Back to us.

3 Sadhguru (@SadhguruJV), "Whenever something hurts you, there are two options: you can either become wounded or you can become wise. This is the choice." X, October 14, 2018, https://x.com/SadhguruJV/status/1051344349030563841.

I fell in love with gymnastics in my front yard. My older niece and cousin would flip from one end of the yard to the next, from my mama's house to my aunt's house, and I was mesmerized. Watching them, I knew I had to learn. That's where my inspiration came from—the raw, backyard kind of gymnastics, where the only coach you had was the dirt beneath your feet.

Eventually, I joined a real gymnastics team, and while the uneven parallel bars were *my jam*, the balance beam? That thing betrayed me. I fell off hard and injured my leg. I knew something was wrong, but what hurt more than my leg was the reaction I got when the hospital bill arrived.

Instead of concern, I got yelled at. I knew money was tight, and my injury added an unexpected expense. My parents made me feel horrible; they acted like I had personally inconvenienced them—which, to be fair, I did. But I was a kid, and instead of feeling supported, I felt like I had committed some *great financial sin*.

That moment stuck with me. To this day, I hate opening mail, and I'd rather tough out an injury than deal with doctors.

But my childhood wounds ran much deeper.

I faced incest and molestation until I finally found the courage to tell my dad. He put an end to it physically, but emotionally, I was still drowning. And my mom? She did nothing. That silence, that indifference, only deepened my feelings of being unwanted and unworthy.

The hurt I held inside from childhood manifested itself in my young adulthood as a woman looking for love and security in the arms of men who couldn't provide it. I had my first child at 19. She was a beautiful baby girl and is an even more gorgeous woman now. I had my second child by my first husband at 20, and he was such a cute little boy with a big nose and undeveloped lungs, but now he is rough around the edges, brilliant, handsome and a responsible husband and father. I went through three marriages—one that lasted five years, another that stretched seventeen years, and then the last one… a blink-of-an-eye three or four months.

A Union Built on Broken Ground

Timothy and I met at church, and in the beginning, everything seemed great. *Or so I thought.* Our marriage lasted seventeen years—a long, painful road filled with betrayal, sprinkled with some laughter here and there, but mostly disrespect, heartbreak, and regret.

Truth be told, we were both unfaithful.

In fact, our relationship began with infidelity—with both of us cheating on our spouses to be with each other. That should've been the first red flag. But I convinced myself that love could grow from broken soil—that somehow, we could build something real on a foundation of lies and betrayal.

I was wrong.

From the start, cheating ran through our marriage like it was written into our vows. From pornography to other women contacting me on social media, I was constantly reminded I wasn't the only one in his world. Women from the church, the same ones who couldn't stand me, slid into my DMs asking if Timothy was divorcing me.

Timothy also had a daughter, but I was never allowed to participate in her life. Before we got married, I was told by Tim and his ex-wife's mother, "She has a mother. She doesn't need you." That hurt lingered, because I cared for her deeply, and there were so many times she wanted me there. But I could only support her *inside our home*—never in public, never outside the walls of our house.

Over time, our relationship became so damaged that even counseling couldn't fix it. Too much had been said, too much had been done. The disrespect was constant, especially in front of other church members, the worship team, and in front of our band members. Tim berated me publicly, regularly, and I had trained myself to ignore it—until one day, a church member finally called him out. He let him know that he was NOT acting Christ-like and he said, "It's really a ugly thing that I see you do repeatedly and God is telling me to tell you to stop."

That moment broke me. The floodgates opened, and for the first time, someone else stood up for me. Someone *saw me*. And for once, I wouldn't be the one left enduring the pain of his fist—because someone else had stepped in first.

One night, Timothy's daughter asked if I could attend an event. I wanted to be there for her, so I asked Tim if I could go.

That's when he snapped.

"Bitch, I hate you, and I'm going to make you pay for what you've done!"

And just like that, something inside me shattered. Not cracked, not dented—full-on, glass-on-concrete, unfixable-level shattered.

Now, let me give you some context before you think I burned his childhood teddy bear or crashed his car. This outburst? It came right after I had cancelled a major contract due to a financial downturn in our business. And why were we taking such a hit? Because of Timothy's illegal business practices. He was out there moving like a villain in a bad crime show, and somehow, I was the problem?

We had a federal subcontract, and Tim—thinking he was the mastermind of a low-budget mob film—decided to dispose of the waste illegally. And guess what? He got caught. That led to a federal investigation, police involvement, and jail time for him. And because of that mess? We lost our bonds and several federal contracts. The worst part was that every single contract was in my name. So when the feds came knocking, they weren't looking for Timothy—they were looking for me.

We had to pay hefty fines and a clean-up fee that nearly wiped out our bank account. Equipment started breaking down because there wasn't enough money for maintenance. The business was crumbling, and I had no one to turn to for help. I handled all the paperwork while Tim was supposed to handle the equipment. And when everything started falling apart, I made the only decision that made sense: I turned the contracts back in because we didn't have the finances to operate safely. A truck had already flipped on Central Ave—what was next? A fatal accident? A lawsuit?

And for that? Tim hated me.

That night, when he called me a bitch, it wasn't just words. It was punishment—for choosing safety, for making a call that went against his ego. For refusing to be complicit in his recklessness. That night didn't just cut deep—it ripped something inside of me that I couldn't put back together.

I was standing there, mind blown, heart racing, adrenaline pumping, trying to process how a man who put our entire business in jeopardy had the audacity—the unmitigated gall—to act like *I* had committed some kind of treason.

Make it make sense.

After I turned in the contract, Tim demanded I get a job to help cover the household bills—because apparently, his mess was still *my* responsibility. Fine. I did what I had to do and started working as a saleswoman for a company in the same industry we were already in.

Within six months, I brought in $15 million in signed contracts. Fifteen. Million. Dollars.

You would think I'd be celebrating, popping champagne, maybe even securing my financial future, right? Wrong. Instead, the owner of the company refused to pay me. Why? Because, according to this insecure, small-minded fool, there was no way I could bring in that much money in that short amount of time without sleeping my way to the top.

Oh, so now competence is suspicious? Now my ability to outperform their entire sales team is too good to be true? I fought like hell for my rightful commission, but when I explained the situation to Tim, expecting at least *some* level of outrage, do you know what he said?

"That's what you get. Karma is a bitch."

After everything—the cheating, the illegal business practices, the financial downfall, the public humiliation—after I single-handedly secured $15 million in contracts, this man still found a way to make it *my* fault?

That moment solidified everything I had been avoiding… That was it. I was done. Tim had spent years tearing me down, and for a long time, I let it happen. I ignored the warnings, the red flags, the blatant disrespect, convincing myself that if I just held on a little longer, endured a little more, it would get better.

It never got better.

Timothy's anger, cheating, and resentment had already written the ending of our marriage long before I finally decided to walk away.

After The Night He Called Me a Bitch

Fifteen years in. Fifteen years of disrespect, infidelity, and abuse. And through it all, I had been faithful. I had never cheated, never stepped outside my marriage—until the night he called me a bitch, and something inside me snapped again. That word wasn't new. Timothy had called me that plenty of times before, flung it at me like a verbal slap whenever he felt like putting me in my place. But this time? This time, it cut different. This time, I didn't just hear it—I felt it *rip through me.*

That same night, still drowning in emotional wreckage, a colleague called about a job I had secured for the company. He must have heard the shattered pieces of me through the phone because he asked where I was and came to check on me. And in that moment—broken, exhausted, done—I let my guard down. We became an item right there in the wreckage of my marriage. And looking back, I realized this was a pattern.

Pain had always been the catalyst for my next move. When life shattered me, I didn't pause to pick up the pieces—I just ran to the next thing, the next distraction, the next person who felt safe in the moment. Abandonment? Betrayal? Disrespect? Instead of sitting in it, healing from it, I sought rescue, validation, a warm body to convince me I still mattered.

I didn't just fall into relationships—I collapsed into them.

Every time a man tore me down, I found another man to build me back up. Or at least, that's what I told myself. The truth? I wasn't healing—I was just finding new band-aids for old wounds, covering fresh scars with borrowed comfort, mistaking proximity for love.

And there I was again. In the arms of someone new, not because I had moved on, but because I had nowhere else to go.

And when I finally confessed? Tim lost it. He beat me so badly he ripped out my braids, leaving bald spots across my scalp. But it didn't stop there. The abuse continued—more fists, more rage, more of him trying to break what was already shattered. There were times I had to call his sister to come save me. Imagine that— having to call your abuser's own family for protection from him.

By the time I finally decided to leave Tim, my escape plan was already in motion. My daughter was coming home from college for the weekend and asked if she could bring a friend. To keep up appearances, I said yes and had to delay. She had no clue about my plans—I had never told my children about the abuse. They didn't know about the bruises, the fear, or the nights I spent questioning my own reality.

I planned to leave right after my daughter and her friend left to return to school. Tim and I shared a king-size bed, but I lay on the farthest edge, trying to create a barrier of nothingness between us. I didn't want his leg to touch me, his breath to reach me—I wanted to disappear.

Then, like clockwork, he tried to initiate sex.

I refused.

It started as a game—a push, a grab, a hand that wouldn't let go. But it wasn't a game to me. My mind and my mouth were screaming NO, but my body betrayed me. And I hated it.

Even though I was mentally resisting, my body had its own response. I wasn't consenting—I was coping. We ended up having sex, but afterward, I felt disturbed, ashamed, and furious with myself.

I had no name for what had just happened—I only knew I felt violated, confused, and broken.

The next morning, I cried out to Daddy, begging for an answer: "Why?! Why did my body betray me when I meant NO?"

And Daddy responded: *The first time you were ever touched, it was taken. And you've continued the cycle—with your actions and your words.*

I froze.

Memories came rushing back like floodwaters—things I had locked away, words I had told myself for years. *If I were ever raped, I would be a rapist's worst nightmare—because I would enjoy it being taken.* That thought had lived in my mind for years, a false sense of empowerment, an attempt to protect myself from my true feelings of powerlessness.

And now? I was watching it play out in real-time.

My body didn't trust me—because my actions had never truly agreed with my words.

The morning I left, I broke down and told my daughter, asking her to come with me. She refused. And that broke me in ways I wasn't prepared for. But I couldn't let it stop me—I had to go. Tears streamed down my face as I drove away, pouring my heart out to my Beloved Daddy because I knew He hated divorce.

And He responded: *But I love you.*

I responded back: *And I am going to fix this.*

I sobbed harder, and Daddy repeated: *I love you.*

Through my brokenness, I whispered back: "I love you too."

Then He hit me with something deeper: *Before you were born, I sent a Savior. You were bankrupt and empty. Receive My love—to overflow and be healed.*

I pleaded, "How?!"

And He answered: *Agree with Me about My love for you.*

In that moment, He showed me on the screen of my mind a four-leaf clover, and a song bubbled up inside me as I imagined myself plucking each leaf—simple, childlike, and freeing: "He loves me/ He loves me so much/ He loves me/ He loves me so much/ He loves me." ("He Loves" by Carmen Calhoun)

The Molecular Structure of Hurt

![The Molecular Structure of Hurt — a diagram with HURT at the center connected to surrounding nodes: PAIN, BITTERNESS, BETRAYAL, AGGRESSIVE, HEARTACHE, ISOLATION, IRRITABLE, EMOTIONAL, HOSTILITY, SUFFERING, VENGEFULNESS, NUMBNESS, RESENTMENT, LOSS, DETACHMENT, ANGER, TRAUMA, ANGUISH]

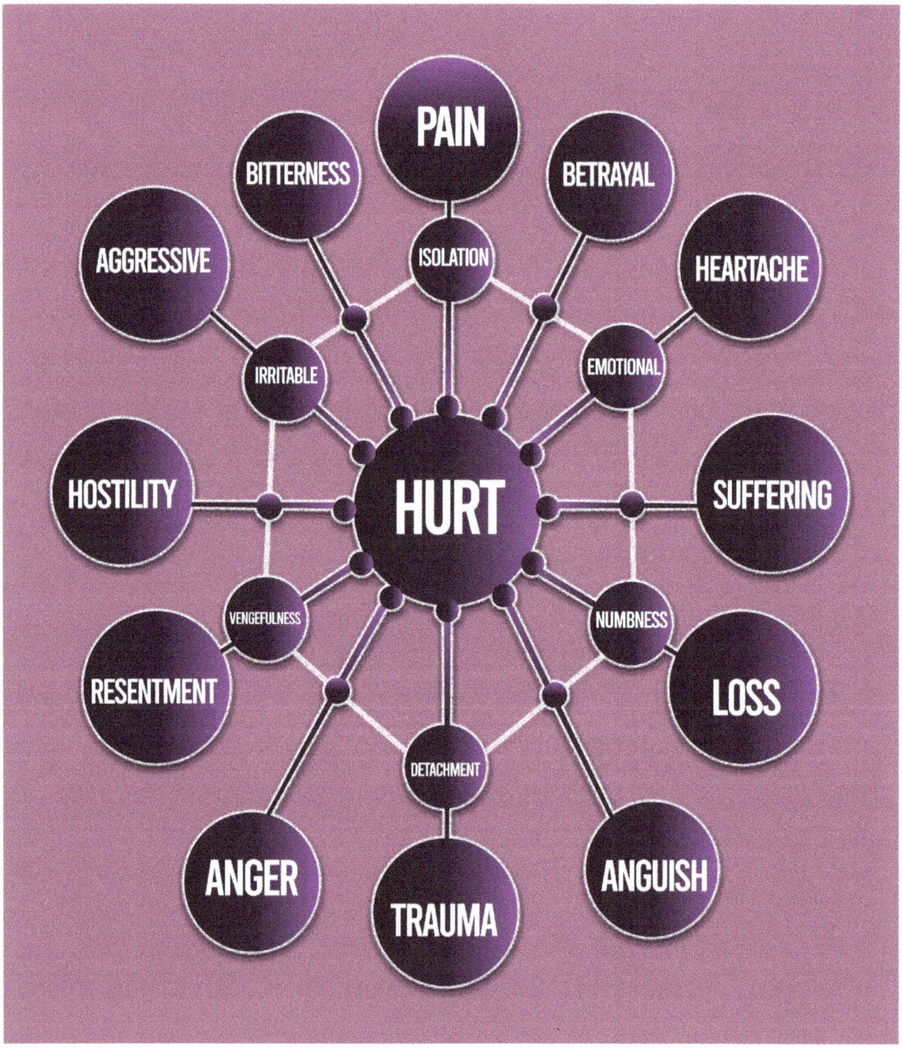

Image created by Sadia Shahid

When you look at how Hurt operates, it's not just a collection of emotions—it's a living, breathing organism that thrives on Pain, Betrayal, and unhealed wounds. Hurt doesn't arrive and leave quietly—it sets up shop, redecorates, and builds a nest in your most vulnerable places. It connects to elements like Anger, Trauma, Bitterness, and Loss, ensuring that what starts as a single wound can spread into a full-blown infection of the heart and mind.

The interconnectedness of Hurt's molecular structure shows how quickly it can take over. Just like in my marriage to Tim, each betrayal I experienced led to Anger, which festered into Bitterness, creating a pathway for Trauma, and setting the stage for perpetual Loss. Each element in the chain was a contributing factor that kept the cycle of Hurt alive and well.

But here's the truth I learned that I want every single human being to know: Hurt doesn't have to be a life sentence. Sometimes, it's the very catalyst that propels us into deep healing. Just like a physical wound that triggers the body's healing response, Hurt can push us to examine our pain, confront our trauma, and find restoration. It challenges us to either hold onto the wound or let Beloved Identity transform it into a scar—a sign of survival and strength.

Hurt can change the script, if you let it. It's the part of the story where you realize that healing isn't about erasing the past but about finding purpose in the pain. How does this happen? By applying radical forgiveness to those who have wounded us and to ourselves.

Breaking the Cycle: Forgiveness, Healing, and Moving Forward

Matthew 18:21-22 (NKJV) says, "Then Peter came to Him and asked, 'Lord, how many times will my brother sin against me, and I forgive him? Up to seven times?' Jesus answered him, 'I say to you, not up to seven times, but seventy times seven.'"

The first time I read this, I got straight-up indignant with God. "What do you mean 70×7?! That's 490 times! Is that per day, a month, a year, or a lifetime?"

I swear I heard a chuckle from heaven—like God was laughing at my little tantrum. And then the Spirit hit me with a truth I wasn't ready for:

It's not that a person actually offends you that many times, but that your mind and your conscience will keep bringing it back up. And every time it comes to you mentally, remind yourself that you have forgiven them.

And just like that, it clicked. Forgiveness isn't a one-time event. It's a process—just like a wedding versus a marriage. A wedding is a single-day event, full of excitement, vows, and celebration. It's the grand moment where you say, "I do!" People clap, you take pictures, and everyone assumes the hard part is over.

But then there's the marriage—the actual commitment; that's where the work begins. Marriage is lived out daily, through love, patience, miscommunication, making up, and choosing each other again and again—especially on the days when you don't feel like it. Forgiveness works the same way. Saying *"I forgive you"* is like the wedding—a declaration, a decision, a moment. But the real work of forgiveness is in marriage—the daily choice to release bitterness when the memory resurfaces, to let go when resentment tries to creep back in, and to remind yourself that you've already chosen peace.

Just like a marriage is tested over time, so is forgiveness—not because you didn't mean it the first time, but because healing is a journey, not a single event. See, I used to think forgiveness was just words—like if I said "I forgive you," then that was it. Case closed.

But I've learned something powerful: Forgiveness is so much bigger than that. Forgiveness is a battle between your heart and your memory. It's telling yourself, "I release this" even when the pain sneaks back up. It's choosing freedom over bitterness—again, and again, and again. Until one day, you wake up and realize...it doesn't hurt anymore.

Forgiveness is more than words. It's actions. It's something, and then it's nothing—but all of it falls under the umbrella of love and grace. "Beloved, I pray that you may prosper in all things and be in health, just as your soul prospers." (3 John 1:2, NKJV). Now, that scripture had me side-eyeing heaven and asking some real questions: What does my soul have to do with my physical well-being? How does my soul prospering impact my health? How does my healing affect my soul?

And over time, I learned something powerful: Healing isn't just about forgiving others—it's about forgiving yourself too. Even the science proves it: In a nationwide study of adults aged 18 and over, those who scored lower on self-forgiveness experienced greater psychological distress and higher levels of depression.[4]

Sometimes you're not consciously aware of how much unforgiveness you're harboring against yourself, but maybe you struggle with chronic, dull depression and nothing seems to help. Perhaps you carry an idealized version of yourself in your

---

4 Berit Ingersoll-Dayton, Cynthia Torges, and Neal Krause, "Unforgiveness, Rumination, and Depressive Symptoms," *Aging & Mental Health* 14, no. 4 (May 2010): 439-49. https://doi.org/10.1080/13607860903483136.

head, and you're disappointed because you feel you haven't been able to live up to it. Maybe you think you're mad at the one who abused you, but when you dig down deeper you're even angrier at yourself for letting it happen and doing nothing to stop it.

Romans 8:1-2 (TPT) issues a powerful declaration against the judgments we level against ourselves: "So now the case is closed. There remains no accusing voice of condemnation against those who are joined in life-union with Jesus, the Anointed One. For the law of the Spirit of life flowing through the anointing of Jesus has liberated us from the law of sin and death."

If God doesn't accuse us, why do we think it's okay to stand as judge and jury over ourselves? It's time to throw that S.H.I.T. overboard! It's time to let God's love flood your being, so when the memories try to creep in, when the ghosts of pain whisper that you're still broken, when the trauma tricks you into believing you haven't moved on—

You remind yourself: I've already been forgiven. *I am forgiven.*

You remind yourself: I've already been healed. *I am healed.*

You align yourself with the truth of who God says you are. You stand in your authority as a child of God and refuse to allow the wreckage of Hurt, Shame, and Self-Hatred to call the shots. You walk in freedom, healing, and a light so bright no darkness can snuff it out.

Forgiveness isn't about pointing fingers or assigning blame—it's about seeing things for what they are. This cycle of pain? It didn't start with you, me, or any one person. It's ancestral, generational, deeply ingrained—passed down like a family heirloom nobody wanted.

But we don't have to carry it forward.

We aren't here to judge, criticize, or shame. We're here to acknowledge, transform, and heal. Our bodies are earthen vessels, clay pots—fragile, yet resilient. If we spend our lives clutching old wounds, we never make space for healing. Many of us repeat the pain we don't resolve. It's a cycle—hurting people hurt people. But the real question is, do we keep the cycle spinning, or do we finally break free?

Papa (God) warns us about holding on to offense in Proverbs 18:19 (NKJV): "A brother offended is harder to win than a strong city, and contentions are like the bars of a castle." Holding onto offense is like building your own prison and locking yourself inside. It's not the offender or the offense that chains you—it's your own decision to stay bound.

And the root of being bound? Unforgiveness. It's the distraction that keeps us separated from one another, from healing, and from peace. But here's the truth—we always have a choice. We can keep picking at old wounds, or we can let the breath of God— His Ruach—flow through us, heal us, and set us free.

Practical Tools for Release

Cold Water Therapy: Resetting the Nervous System. Cold exposure increases dopamine (the motivation chemical) and reduces stress response. Try this: Take a 30-second cold shower or splash cold water on your face when feeling triggered. This helps break the loop of trauma responses.

Journaling: Print out an invoice and list out all of the offenses that come to mind. Pray over each one, releasing them to God and saying out loud, "I forgive you." Once you are done, write the word PAID over the middle of the paper.

Affirmations: Stand in front of the mirror and declare: "My Hurt is part of my story, but it does not define me. I am whole. I am healed."

Community: Surround yourself with safe people who hold space for your healing and celebrate your growth.

Visualization: Close your eyes and imagine carrying a cargo box marked "Hurt" and throwing it overboard. What does it feel like to let it go?

Music for Meditation:
"Safe" by Jon Waller, performed by Carmen Calhoun

Chapter Three

INSECURITY IN IRONS

Listen, I have to tell on myself. I was the queen of relationship performances—standing center stage, lights on, audience of one: *him.*

For seven, whole, years, I was entangled with this man. Seven years—that's a bachelor's degree and a master's if you do summer classes—and still, I didn't have a key to his house. Here's the gag: The first two years, I didn't even know I was playing a co-star to someone else's movie. Yep, I didn't know he had a whole other relationship—a full-on, living, breathing, "Hi, I'm his girlfriend" situation while I'm over here making chicken cacciatore and rubbing feet like I'm in a Nicholas Sparks novel.

The insecurity? Oh, baby, it pulled up a chair and unpacked its suitcase. I became Betty Crocker, Erykah Badu, and Tabitha Brown rolled into one. Cooking? Done. Massaging? Done. Sexing? Honey, I did it like I was running for *Employee of the Month.* I covered every base, convinced that if I just gave enough, loved hard enough, twisted it up enough in the sheets—surely, *surely,* he'd come to his senses and hand me a key. Not even a big key. I would've settled for the spare one, you know, the little ugly one you tape under the flowerpot. But no. Nada.

The joke was on me. And the joke was fed by Insecurity dressed up as love.

Because the truth is, deep down I believed if I wasn't everything to him, I would be nothing to him. See, I was trying to win a game I didn't even know I was playing. I thought I was auditioning for wife. Turns out I was playing convenient comfort while he took intermissions with other women.

The Insecurity? Oh, it was loud: "Maybe if you just do a little more.

Maybe if you just stay a little longer. Maybe if you prove you're better than the other one. Maybe if you season the food *just right*, he'll put a ring on it *and* give you a key." Y'all, I was making rosemary-infused lamb chops like I was on *Chopped*, and this man still had me standing outside the house like I was Amazon Prime delivery. And it wasn't even just him—it was ME. I was holding the apron, the massage oil, and the body heat hostage like it was going to make him love me. When in reality, I had already handed him the blueprint that said: "You don't actually have to give me what I want, I'll stay anyway."

Oof. Performing. Over-functioning. Calling Insecurity "patience" when it was actually self-abandonment. And before you judge me too hard, let's keep it all-the-way real: How many of us have been out here baking casseroles for men who won't even share their Netflix password, much less a mortgage? I wasn't waiting on a key. I was avoiding the truth: that I didn't trust I could get what I actually wanted, that I feared walking away more than I feared staying miserable, that I thought "doing the most" would finally make me enough.

But listen here: You can't screw, sauté, or spa-treatment your way into commitment. Love is a *choice*—not a reward you get after winning The Relationship Olympics. And the most tragic part? I was so busy working for love I didn't even notice I was living without it.

If you recognize yourself here…You ain't crazy. You ain't stupid. You've just been sailing the ship of Insecurity, hoping that if you decorate it well enough, it'll float into the harbor of being chosen. But baby, that ship is leaking, and it's time to throw that S.H.I.T. overboard.

* * *

I've been married not once, not twice, but three whole times—each time hoping, praying, maybe even *bargaining*, that THIS time would be the one where I wouldn't be left shipwrecked at sea, clutching a broken plank called "At least I tried."

In my first marriage, he told me he just needed some space. And what did I say? "Don't be gone too long." Let me tell you what's not funny—he was already gone before he packed a bag. I married a man who was mean to me before the wedding cake even got cut.

But you know me—Captain Save-A-Ho. I thought if I just stayed sweet, cooked the meals, and took the licks (not punches, but the emotional ones), somehow it would turn into love. Instead? He came back and forth like a bad cable signal. And he had the audacity to interrogate my toddler like he was a pint-sized private investigator: "What did Mommy do to you today?"

This toddler couldn't even spell "manipulation" but was out here making up stories on demand like a little Stephen King. And me? I stayed. Watched him punch holes in the walls, watched my kids hide behind couches like it was the apocalypse. And you wanna know the gut punch? My daughter, years later, swore he was hitting me.

But I don't even remember—and maybe that's the most tragic part: I don't remember. Because sometimes, when survival is the assignment, memory checks out and leaves you on autopilot.

My second marriage was a straight-up war zone dressed up in Sunday Best. The man had a PhD in cheating, lying, hitting, and *raping*. But me? I was sitting up in church like a good soldier saying, "God hates divorce." So I stayed. I stayed while my kids grew up watching things no child should watch. I stayed while pornography ran rampant in the house, while secrets became our wallpaper. Not because I was weak—but because I thought God was holding me hostage.

But let me tell you about God's voice. When I finally hit rock bottom, when I was bankrupt—emotionally, spiritually, financially—God didn't scold me.

God didn't shame me.

God whispered: *But I love you.* And that love? Soft. Gentle. Non-religious.

It broke me open. I said: "I love you too."

And the Holy Spirit, cool as ever, said: *You are bankrupt and empty, but before you even knew you needed a Savior, I sent Jesus. BE FILLED TO OVERFLOW.*

That wasn't churchy. That was my lifeline.

By the time #3 came, I already knew he wasn't the one. I knew it. I knew it when he called. I knew it when he kissed me. I knew it while I was still dealing with the debris from marriage #2. But there I was, just hoping maybe he'd be the one to finally choose me—even if I had to shrink into a version of myself I didn't recognize. And yep, he beat me. He punched me. He didn't love me. But somehow, I convinced myself that *love could be negotiated.*

Spoiler: It can't.

But wait, there's more. Let's not act like I didn't try to remix the cycle with extra tracks. Right now? I got two more men in orbit like I'm running a reality TV show. Man #1 is still withholding the house key like it's the Ark of the Covenant. Man #2—we do business together, and somewhere along the way, I lied to him, cheated on him, and excused it because it was easier than telling the truth.

If I'm being honest, I sabotage sometimes. I don't just attract chaos—I participate. I find myself making excuses for what I don't want to do, when I could just open my mouth and tell the truth. But for years, my inner child has been terrified that truth means abandonment, rejection, punishment, and shame.

So instead, I do what good, insecure little girls who grew up surviving do—I make myself small, I make excuses, I try to *control the uncontrollable*, and I call it *being strong.* The edgy truth?

This ain't about the men.

This ain't about the marriages.

This is about the unfinished business I've had with myself, with the little girl who was molested, shamed, dismissed, and left to fend for herself emotionally, while pretending like strength meant ignoring her own needs. But guess what?

> I'm done auditioning.
> I'm done waiting for keys, rings, or holy approval stamps.
> I'm done performing at the altars of Insecurity disguised
> as relationships.

I know God loves me—that's never been the question.
But me? Loving *myself?*
I'm still learning how.
I'm learning to agree with God about me—
    about who I am,
    about what I carry,
    about what I *deserve.*
Right now, I'm empty—and maybe that's grace.
Because empty means there's finally room…

Room to be filled, not just with His love, but with love for myself, too.

The Molecular Structure of Insecurity

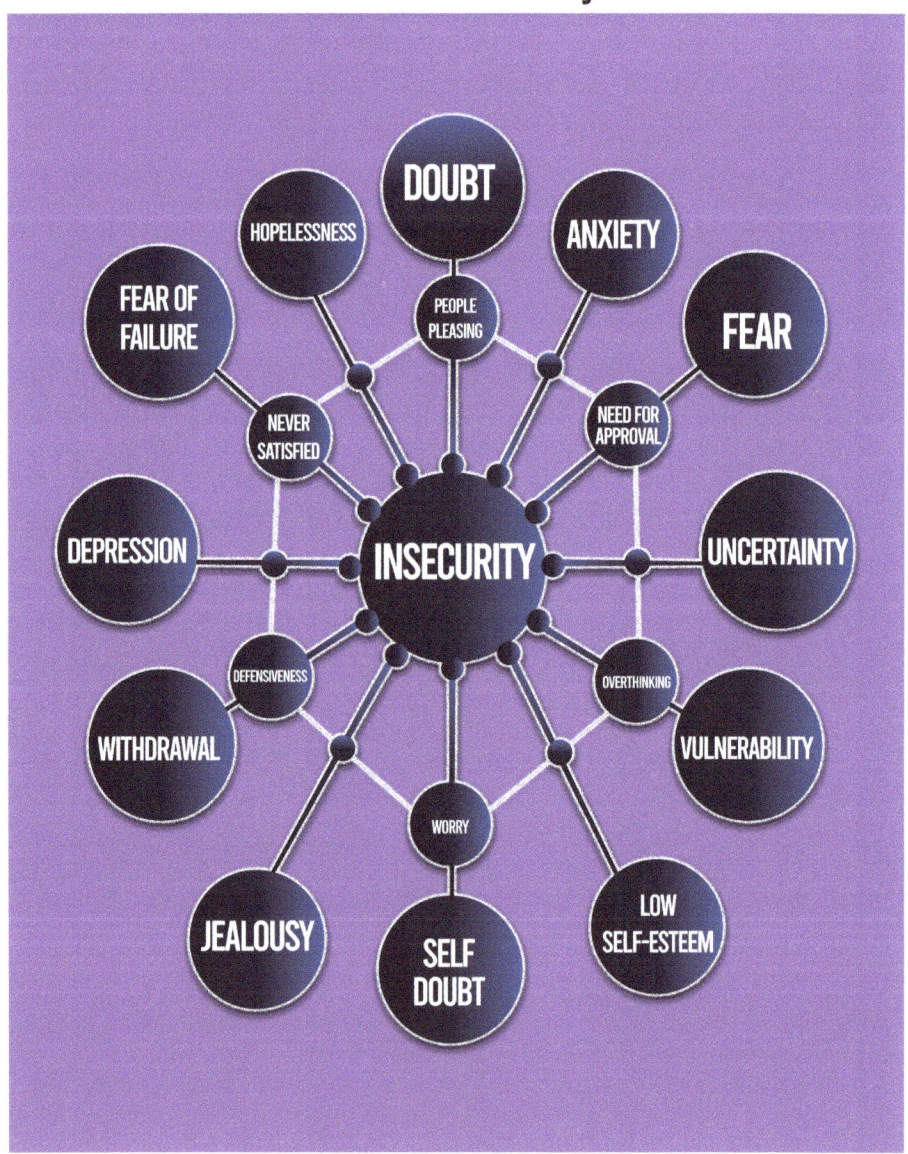

Image created by Sadia Shahid

Insecurity: Oh, that shady little gremlin. It's the voice that asks, "Am I good enough? Do I even matter?" and then snickers in the background while you spiral into Self-Doubt. Insecurity is a con artist, convincing you that your worth is determined by outside validation. But if you depend on others to constantly reassure you, you're basically giving out emotional landlord rights to people who may not even pay rent.

Insecurity isn't just a web of doubts and fears. It's a carefully woven net designed to keep you tangled in a cycle of Uncertainty, Fear of Failure, and Anxiety. Insecurity isn't a one-hit wonder— it's the background music of every negative thought, setting the rhythm for Manipulation, Low Self-esteem, and a never-ending struggle with Vulnerability. At its core, Insecurity is the puppeteer, pulling the strings that keep us small, safe, and stuck.

The interconnectedness of Insecurity's molecular structure shows how quickly it can take over. A single seed of Doubt can sprout into a full-grown forest of Anxiety, its roots spreading into Fear, Withdrawal, and even Jealousy. Before you know it, Insecurity has you questioning your worth, your decisions, and whether you deserve to take up space at all.

But here's the truth: Insecurity doesn't have to be a life sentence. Sometimes, it's the very nudge you need to dig deeper and find your true Beloved Identity. Just like a cracked foundation forces you to rebuild, Insecurity can reveal where your Self-Worth needs fortifying. It pushes you to examine your beliefs, challenge old narratives, and decide whether you'll keep living under its shadow or step into your own light. Insecurity can lead you down the grinding path of performance until you learn that the only approval you need is from the person staring back at you in the mirror.

Insecurity and the Isms

One of the ways insecurity manifests in our lives is through the "Ism Constructs." Racism, sexism, colorism, and all their divisive counterparts are subtle, hypnotic and fear-based. At their core, they are illusions designed to keep us trapped in limitation, convincing us that our worth, potential, and identity are at the mercy of external forces. These constructs plant seeds of division in our minds, nurturing them with whispers of fear: *The white man won't let me prosper. Black people can't be trusted. Spanish people are taking our jobs. The Chinese are outsmarting us*, and so on, and so on, until these thoughts take root and grow into narratives we defend with unwavering fervor.

And we don't just defend them, we argue for them. We debate the validity of our limitations to the fifth degree, recounting story after story to prove why our struggles are inevitable and why the system is rigged against us. We carry these arguments into our conversations, our communities, and even our own hearts, reinforcing the very chains we long to break.

Let's address some of the common "Isms"—racism, colorism and pretty ideology—and their impact on our sense of security and well-being.

Racism: Subtle and Insidious

Racism's most harmful effects often lie in the subtle, everyday experiences—microaggressions, stereotypes, and dismissals. These moments may seem insignificant individually but, over time, create a cumulative burden that erodes mental well-being and self-worth. A casual comment about being "surprisingly articulate" or an assumption based on race can have profound long-term effects. Focusing only on overt racism ignores the quieter harm that deeply impacts individuals and communities.

Colorism: Internalized Division

Colorism functions similarly, reinforced through quiet preferences for lighter skin in families, media, and social structures. Comments like, "You're so pretty for a dark-skinned girl" or the favoritism shown to lighter-skinned individuals perpetuate a hierarchy that damages self-perception. For those impacted, it creates Insecurity and internalized Shame. For those who benefit, it imposes pressures to conform, fostering disconnection from identity. These experiences, compounded over time, divide communities and hinder collective progress.

Pretty: The Narrow Standard

The "pretty" construct, tied to Eurocentric beauty ideals, subtly defines worth through physical appearance. Everyday exposure to media, cultural norms, and biased compliments reinforces narrow standards, causing individuals to internalize self-doubt and comparison. The harm is not from overt rejection but the accumulation of unspoken messages about what is deemed valuable.

* * *

What ties these constructs together is their ability to persist unnoticed until their impact is undeniable. The fear-based nature of these constructs thrives on emotional energy. Each time we repeat, *"The white man won't let me prosper,"* we reinforce a narrative of helplessness. Each time we say, *"If my skin was lighter, I would get the job,"* we deepen the divide within our own community. Each time we think, *"If I was thinner I would be lovable,"* we support a toxic belief system that connects a number on a scale to a woman's worth. These whispers are the tools of fear, designed to keep us fighting one another instead of dismantling the system itself.

But fear, by its very nature, is a deceiver. It creates the illusion of powerlessness, masking the truth that these constructs are human-made, not divine mandates. They are not immutable laws of existence but frameworks built to divide and control. And yet, we cling to them because fear feels familiar—it justifies our anger, our pain, and our sense of injustice. It gives us something to point to, something to blame. But blaming the 'isms' doesn't free us; it binds us.

So, what if we stopped? What if we questioned these whispers? What if we dared to believe that they are nothing more than false evidence appearing real? The truth is, the moment we stop giving these constructs our energy, they lose their power. Yes, racism, sexism, and other 'isms' exist, and yes, their effects are real—but they are not all-powerful. They are constructs, not truths. And what is constructed can be deconstructed, first within ourselves and then in the world around us.

The first step to breaking free is recognizing the lie. Fear tells us, *You'll never succeed because of them.* But truth says, *You were created with the power to thrive, no matter the odds.* Fear says, *They are the reason you can't move forward.* But truth says, *You can move forward when you stop believing the whispers of division.* Fear thrives on scarcity and division, while truth invites us into abundance and unity.

I dare you to ask yourself: *Who would I be if I stopped believing the whispers? What could I accomplish if I chose not to participate in the hypnotism of fear? What might my life look like if I believed in the infinite possibilities of my existence instead of the limitations imposed by the 'isms'?"*

The moment we stop arguing for our limitations, the chains begin to loosen. The whispers lose their power. The constructs begin to crumble. And in their place, we find something greater: freedom. Freedom to see each other as human beings, not adversaries. Freedom to live beyond fear. Freedom to prosper, not because of anyone else's permission, but because it is our divine birthright. Fear may whisper, but the truth will always speak louder if we have the courage to listen.

The Light and the Pearl

Now that we've heard the many dark voices of Insecurity, let's change up the station and tune into what Papa says about us. According to Him, we are carriers of divine light, uniquely created with personalities, preferences, and peculiarities that display His radiance. 2 Corinthians 4:6 (MIRROR) says, "The same God who made light shine out of darkness has kindled a light in our hearts, whose shining is to make known his glory as he has revealed it in the features of Jesus Christ."

Imagine a pilot light inside every human being. Our faith in Jesus is the fuel source that causes our lights to shine. And here's the thing: We never know on this side of heaven how our light impacts the world. We may be aware of how the lights in those around us inspire us and illuminate our path, but trust me on this: Your existence and your divine radiance matters to many more people than you even realize!

If we continue into verse seven of the same passage above, we see that the source of our light is God Himself: "And now, in the glow of this glorious light and with unveiled faces we discover this treasure where it was hidden all along, in these frail skin-suits made of clay. We did not invent ourselves; we are God's idea to begin with and the dynamic of his doing and amazing engineering. (The word translated earthen vessel or clay jar is the word ostrakinos from ostrakon, 'oyster').")

Just like the internal pilot light, the oyster is another great word picture for how we carry a treasure within us. The value of the oyster shell's exterior can never compete with the valuable pearl it holds inside. There is so much more to you than what meets the eye. "The kingdom of heaven is like treasure hidden in a field. When a man found it, he hid it again, and then in his joy went and sold all he had and bought that field" (Matthew 13:44, NIV). You are the field AND the treasure!

In order to renew our minds from the lies we believe about ourselves, God invested all he has in redeeming our original value. He reinstated our original design. Our beings hold this treasure, the original blueprint of our innocent humanity. Jesus said in John 7:37-38 (MIRROR), "In your realizing that I am what the Scriptures are all about, you will discover uniquely for yourself, face to face with me, that *I am what you are all about* and rivers of living waters will gush out of your innermost being."

Breaking the Bonds of Insecurity

Freedom from Insecurity is not about becoming fearless—it's about embracing Vulnerability as a strength. Accepting the truth about our Beloved Identity is the mirror that reflects truth instead of lies. Through practices like breathwork, affirmations, and intentional community, Insecurity loses its hold, allowing confidence, peace, and inner rest to take its place.

Practical Tools for Release

Breathwork: Inhale acceptance, exhale Insecurity. Each breath is a reminder that you are enough.

Journaling: Write down the lies Insecurity has told you and rewrite them with declarations of truth.

Affirmations: Stand in front of the mirror and declare: "I am worthy. I am loved. I am enough."

Community: Surround yourself with voices that speak life and truth, reinforcing your Beloved Identity.

Music for Meditation

"Dare 2 Be You" by Carmen Calhoun

Chapter Four

TACKING THROUGH TROUBLE

Trouble is the inevitable outcome when we refuse to deal with our Shame, Hurt, and Insecurities. It's the storms of our own making when we operate unconsciously out of old wounds. Sometimes the trouble seems to creep in unnoticed, other times it crashes down like a rogue wave as a result of our poor choices. Trouble never travels alone; it arrives with its entourage: Misery, Danger, Disruption, and Instability. Together, they conduct the kind of chaos that leaves us feeling lost, confused, and grasping for stability.

Trouble shows up in overdue bills, empty refrigerators, and the quiet, heavy air of a household weighed down by gambling habits and drug addiction. Trouble turns the kitchen table from a place of connection into a battleground of bitterness and unmet expectations.

But Trouble isn't simply a financial outcome; it's an emotional and spiritual one. It is the chaos we welcome into our world when we don't listen to our bodies, our intuition, or the still, small voice of the Holy Spirit.

Like, for example, what I did marrying my last husband. *Whew.* I knew better, ignored my gut, and married Marc—a colleague who was nothing more than a distraction from my last heartbreak.

But before Marc was ever in my life, before I made the mistake of marrying him, I had an unforgettable run-in with *her*—my co-worker, Casey, who would later have an affair with Marc.

Y'all, I tried to be nice to this girl. Every morning I walked into work in my own little praise-and-worship bubble, singing in my head, keeping my spirit light. "Goooooood morning, Williamson Paving!" (Think of "Good morning, Vietnam" with Robin Williams.) I would often surprise the office by cooking either breakfast or lunch without asking for a dime just to show them love. When I came in every morning I greeted every single person with a grand hello, a wave if my colleagues were on the phone, and sometimes a song, but always with a smile, including Casey. But no matter how much kindness I dished out, she stayed miserable.

One day, as the phones rang off the hook, I walked back to her office and asked, "Can you please help answering the phones?"

Casey snapped, "Get out of my face, Carmen!"

Wait, what?! I repeated, "Just answer the phone."

She got up and slammed the door in my face.

Oh. Okay. So that's where we're at now? I was still floating in my happy place (delusionally happy, maybe, but happy nonetheless). Still grinning like I had good sense, I turned my face toward my supervisor—who sat in the office right next to hers—and called out between laughs, "You betta come get her!"

I was casually walking away, still amused, when suddenly—I heard it. The wind shifted. That unmistakable *whoosh* of pure rage, the sound of a door handle being yanked with unnecessary force. *Oh, we doing THIS?*

Before I could fully process the situation, Casey stormed out of her office like she was auditioning for WWE, got right up in my face, and with her chest all puffed up, she yelled, "And what are YOU gonna do about it, Carmen?" She pushed against me repeatedly like she forgot I was raised in a house where "move me if you bad" was a real-life challenge.

At first, I laughed. I mean, surely, she had lost her damn mind. My brain short-circuited for a second, trying to comprehend the audacity. I thought, *Girl, you have no idea who you're dealing with. I am a church girl—but a church girl gone wild.* That's the thing people don't realize: "Church girls" don't mean we won't fight, it just means we'll pray about it after.

Then something snapped. My mind flooded with every single time this crazy woman had been nasty to me and others for no reason, and before I knew it—I whipped her ass. No hesitation, no second thoughts, just pure, "You got the right one today" energy. I backed her straight into her office, giving her that work.

My supervisor ran in to break it up—I raised my hand to hit her again, and he caught my arm, but let's be real—he went with it. My adrenaline was pumping, and for a split second, I swear he was debating whether to let me land just one more for good measure. It was giving, "I gotta do this for HR, but I low-key support it."

As I walked to the door to leave her office, I turned to her and said, "Don't you EVER disrespect me like that again," slammed her door, and kept moving like I had somewhere to be and no regrets.

News spread like wildfire. My field coworkers were calling in, saying, "Ms. Carmen, is that you?" I said "Yes," and they hit me with, "Thank you so very much," before hanging up like I had just handled community business. Of course, I still got called into the office. The owner—a beautiful man who looked at me like he got it but still had to act like he didn't—leaned back in his chair, rubbing his temples like he was debating whether this was really worth the paperwork. But Casey's aunt, the office manager? She was DONE. Arms crossed, lips pursed, giving me that classic *'Lord, give me strength before I lay hands'* church mother glare. If disappointment had a face, it was hers. I really thought I was about to be escorted out with my purse and a final paycheck, but instead? Two-day suspension. That's it. I was shocked. But let me tell you this—I apologized and moved forward. Not for her, but for me.

And then, years later, she had an affair with my husband.

The Cost of Ignoring My Gut

Let's talk about Marc—the man I should have never married. He was a distraction, a rebound, a lesson I didn't need to learn the hard way—yet somehow, I did. We dated off and on for a few years, and he and my family convinced me to marry him, which was ultimately my decision and I take full responsibility. His kids moved in, his baby mama kept things chaotic, and his weed and drug habit? That only made his manic episodes worse.

Our marriage was a disaster from the jump. I called my girlfriend and asked her to research how I could annul it on our honeymoon—that's how bad it was. But manipulation is a hell of a drug. His jealousy, his dependency, the suffocating control—it was all too much. It was my wedding day, and as my makeup artist painted my face, I heard the Holy Spirit clear as day: *You don't have to do this. Don't do this!*

Now, let me tell you, it wasn't some vague feeling, no whisper-in-the-wind type of thing—nah, this was loud, direct, and sitting in my spirit like an uninvited guest at the reception. But my mind? Oh, my mind immediately went to the crowd—the guests, the food, the dresses, the money spent. The place was packed! People had flown in, outfits had been coordinated, wigs had been secured—chile, this was a full production!

We were getting married at my cousin's bar, Levar's Place—a spot with deep family history, a place my grandmother once owned when I was a baby. A place where more folks had been thrown out than walked down an aisle. And still, I went through with it.

Because what was I supposed to do? Just stand up mid-contour, throw the brush down, and yell, "EVERYBODY GO HOME! GOD SAID NAH?" Imagine that. Aunties clutching their pearls, cousins looking at me like I had lost my damn mind, my children proudly walking me down the aisle "just 'cause we already here."

So instead of listening to the Holy Spirit, I listened to the pressure, the expectations, the "well, we already this far in" logic that gets so many of us caught up. I ignored my gut and walked straight into the storm.

Then came the final straw, a short couple of months later. I had returned from a singing gig out of town, exhausted but relieved to be home. Marc was supposed to pick me up from the airport—and, of course, he was late and drunk. I was mad as fire but kept quiet while he ranted, his words slurring, his attitude nasty. Then he said something—something that hit me the wrong way. Before I knew it, I slammed my hand against the dashboard of his truck. And that's when it turned physical. He took his fist and landed it on the left side of my face. That was it for me, and yet I still tried to help him maintain his business. I did it so I didn't have to fear retaliation.

Then, after being married for just four months and filing for divorce, the owner of the company I worked for pulled me aside and said, "I heard you're getting a divorce because of Casey."

I was totally shocked—I didn't have a clue, so how did *he* know? Before I could even respond, he pulled me in for a hug and said, "You are an incredible woman."

But that wasn't the only conversation we needed to have. I

had to let him know that Marc was threatening my life. He had been going around telling everyone—from truck drivers to repair shops—that he was going to kill me, showing people the gun he possessed. And her? Casey kept him on payroll, still contracting him for work knowing what he was saying.

I showed the owner the text messages as proof that she was still giving him work despite the threats. He looked at me and said, "Don't worry about a thing." And just like that—Marc never worked for the company again.

Years later, I got the news that Marc had shot his girlfriend, then turned the gun on himself. The world reacted in shock, but I sat in gratitude—not for his end, but for my escape. I am the woman who survived. The girl who got away.

It could have ended differently, and for that I have to thank God for His grace. I threw the door open for disaster and instability from that first moment I ignored my intuition. Trouble came in and had a field day with me and it could have cost me my life.

The Molecular Structure of Trouble

Trouble isn't some abstract concept—it's a slow-burn setup for disaster. One moment of Conflict spirals into Struggle, which breeds Misery, and suddenly, you're drowning in Difficulty, clinging to Panic like a life raft and making Hasty Decisions that lead to bad outcomes. And the worst part? You might not even realize that you set the whole thing in motion because of your unresolved Shame, Hurt and Insecurities.

I certainly didn't realize that my relationship with Marc would open the door to Chaos, Stress, and life-threatening Danger, but looking back, I should have been wiser. Small decisions made early on can open the door for Trouble to do its dirty work: keeping you from thriving in peace, joy and purpose.

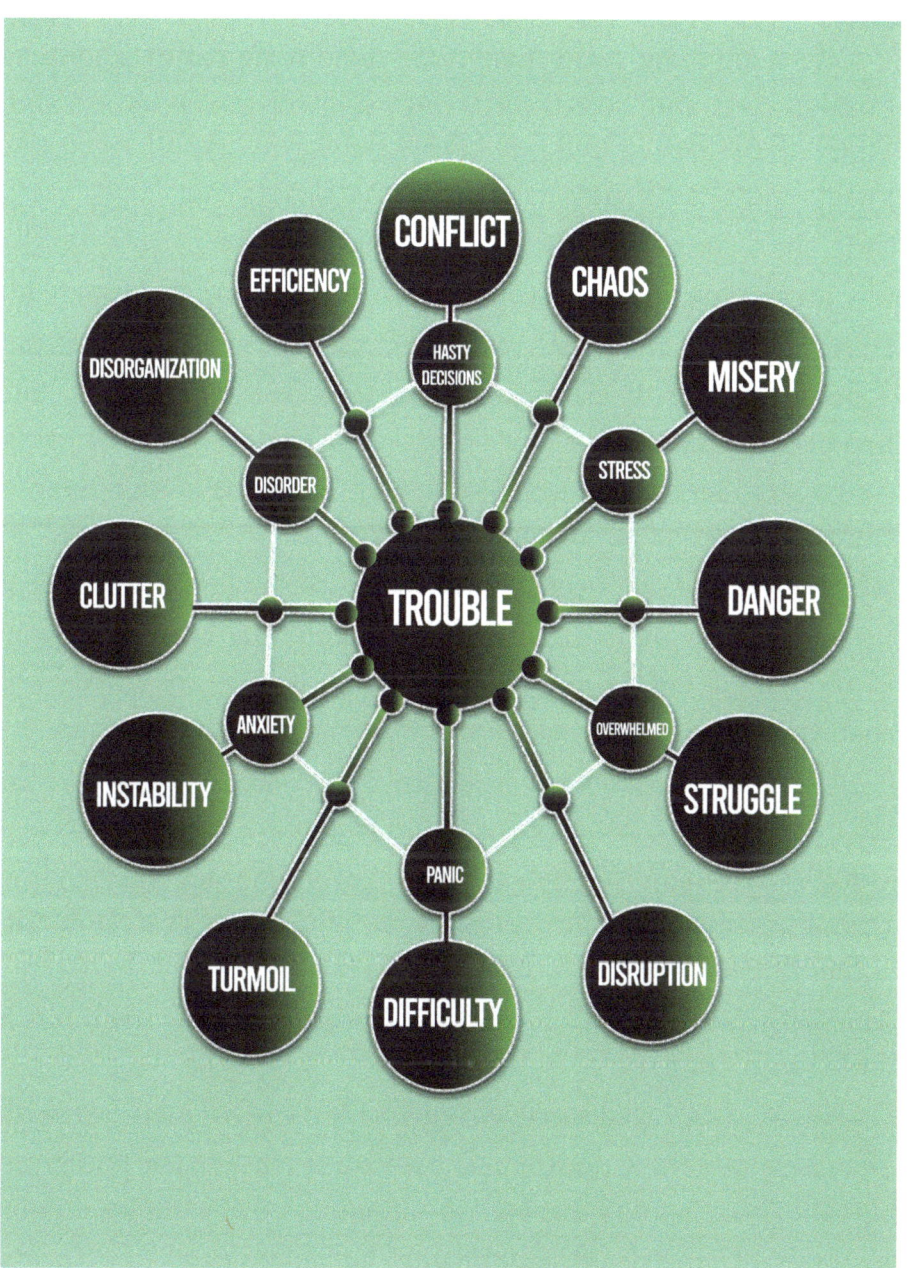

Image created by Sadia Shahid

* * *

The Trouble with Unprocessed Trauma

Mom and Dad were gone, and life twisted into a loop of hospital runs and doctor visits with and for our sister, Deidra. Older than Nareta and me, Deidra often made life difficult. Deidra and I had drifted apart over the years, but when I was little, she was my favorite. My second mother. She was light. She was everything. But life shifted, and that warmth became cold. I used to think she was just mean, and she could be—but her Trouble came from pain and trauma she never processed. She had been abused too.

I remember the day clearly—we were all sitting on our parents' front screened-in porch, grown now, when a memory surfaced for Deidra, and she began to open up. She shared that she had been sexually assaulted, and when she told our mother, instead of receiving comfort, she was met with a beating. She had been shamed not only by a predator, but by our very own mother.

The pain in her voice was raw. Her tears were fresh, like the wound had been reopened just yesterday. I was stunned—completely caught off guard. I had no idea she was carrying all of that. I just assumed she was mean as hell. But at that moment, something shifted. Everything made sense—the way she treated our mother, the drinking, the self-sabotage, the walls she built. It all fell into place.

Nareta and I genuinely loved Deidra and wanted her well. Watching our sister decline was painful. It felt like she had given up. Still, Nareta and I showed up—not from guilt, but love. Each visit was a chance to shine light into her shadows.

Unprocessed trauma really does affect the body—storms you don't even know are brewing wreak havoc in your very bones. It reminds me of that scripture in Proverbs 17:22 (NIV): "A cheerful heart is good medicine, but a crushed spirit dries up the bones." Deidra and I experienced basically the same thing, but our choices took us into different encounters with Trouble. I tried drinking, and after one major hangover, I said, "Nope! Not for me." I never ventured into major drugs, but I had my own vices. I was a little ho back in the day—promiscuous, as the old folks would say.

I wish I knew then what I know now. But life doesn't offer do-overs, just lessons. And every tear Deidra shed on that porch was a reminder of the storms she had weathered alone, and how desperately I wished I could have walked through them with her.

It didn't matter how mad Deidra may have been or how bad she may have treated us—when she needed us, we were there. I purchased so much holistic medicine from Pure Wellness World (www.purewellnessworld.com). I called the owner of the apothecary, Tania Poland, and told her my sister's symptoms, and she curated medicine for Deidra. Deidra said she felt better, but she didn't continue to take it. She called Nareta "Nurse Love" because Nareta made sure Deidra took her medicine, had food to eat, and actually ate what she cooked. (Nareta isn't a nurse by trade, but she sure is in spirit.)

One afternoon, I brought Deidra some Depends. When I walked in, the house was cold. The pellet stove was off. I smelled urine. When I opened her bedroom door, the heat slapped me in the face. Deidra was slumped off the side of the bed, one breath away from hitting the floor.

I froze. Then entered with my usual, "Hey gurl, hey."

She smiled weakly, "Thanks, Carmelita."

I asked if I could clean her up.

"No, I'll get up later," she said.

But I couldn't leave her like that. "Dee," I said softly, "you know I can't leave you here like this."

She finally agreed.

I pushed my leg against the bed, bracing myself, trying to steady her so she wouldn't fall. The urine had saturated everything—the sheets and the mattress were soaked—and the wetness hit my skin, seeping through my clothes. Deidra was skin and bones, yet heavy—hollow. She had been starving herself.

When I tried to lift her, she screamed. A guttural, piercing scream. I ran to get her grandson. By the time we returned, she was on the floor.

We managed to get her up. I called Nareta.

She talked to Deidra on speaker: "We need to get you somewhere that can help, sis."

And just like that, Deidra said, "Okay."

The paramedics arrived, and her oxygen was at 78; her blood pressure was unreadable. Nareta stayed on the phone the whole time. "I love you, Dee. You're going to get better. Carmen and I will be with you every step."

She never came home again.

She went to the hospital and then was transferred to a rehab facility. Her roommate, Ms. J, pulled us aside: "Whatever you do, get her out of here." The place was neglectful. The food was garbage. The staff was slow and distant.

Nareta and I had been on a mission—to love Deidra, to show up for her, to be present. But that night, it felt like she was letting us, really letting us. And that meant everything. She didn't fight us. She let Nareta shampoo and condition her hair, sitting there with a quiet surrender. Nareta worked gently, dipping the wash rag into the pail of water over and over, making sure every trace of shampoo was out. That was just who she was—tender, patient, full of a love that didn't rush.

As I watched her massage the moisturizer into Deidra's thin curls, I couldn't help but think of Mom. The way Deidra's curls tightened, just like Mom's used to, made my heart ache in a way I wasn't ready for. The resemblance, the care, the moment itself—it was too much and just enough, all at the same time.

I probably didn't have to say it, but I did—because it was the truth sitting heavy in my chest. I wished we didn't have to be there like that. I wished sickness hadn't been the current of Trouble that pulled us back into the same waters, forcing us to navigate it together. Sickness had a way of forcing family to show up in ways that health never did. It was cruel like that—demanding presence where life once allowed distance. And I refused to let regret dock itself in that space. I felt a bond we hadn't had in a long time. I couldn't change the past. I couldn't rewrite the years.

But I was there. In that moment. With love.

That night, all of us sisters came together in that little shared space with her. Two of us physically there, and Shayla and Selina through FaceTime. Selina asked, "Do you need anything?" And Deidra, in true Deidra fashion, responded, "No, I'm okay." But here was the shocker: "I have my two sisters here with me—Carmelita and Nurse Love!" Nareta and I both looked at each other in disbelief and smiled.

And just like that, the room filled with laughter. The kind that felt like a deep exhale. The kind that made even the hardest moments lighter. I wished we didn't have to be there. But it was where we needed to be. And I loved her so much.

That night, Deidra made me feel appreciated, and I hadn't even known I needed it. I had to throw my S.H.I.T. overboard so I could be fully present.

And I was so glad I did.

The Call to Disengage and Live

When Deidra was in the ICU in her last week of life, her organs were functioning—but she wasn't there. They ran MRIs. No seizures. Adjusted fluids. Checked vitals. I was waiting on something more than numbers. I wanted a sign of her spirit fighting back.

I called my other sister, Nareta, trying to process, and felt like I upset her. Mid-conversation, I heard it: *Disengage.*

Holy Spirit. Clear as day.

So I paused. Listened.

Later, I called a friend, venting about Deidra's son. How could he not be there? How could he not hold her hand? Then again, the Spirit cut through: *Disengage.*

This time, I snapped back at the Holy Spirit. "I AM ANGRY!"

But Spirit was steady. *You're creating an internal storm. Trouble of your own making. Disengage now. Breathe. Quiet the storm before it wreaks havoc in your body. Take a page from your own book, and throw that S.H.I.T. overboard.*

I shook. But I listened. I took several deep breaths—inhale… exhale. Slow. Steady. Then I spoke life over Deidra. Over her son. I let the storm go.

* * *

We all carry storms within—trauma, shame, pain we've never spoken. Some storms scream. Some fester in silence. But if we don't face them, they'll take us out.

And this is your call. Disengage now—before it's too late. Your body will keep the score. Your lungs will collapse under the weight of what you refuse to release. But healing is still available.

Breathe.

Release.
Live.

The Storms We Carry

Disengage from what is breaking you down so you can engage in what is building you up. Because your trouble does not have to consume you.

Because you deserve to heal.

Because this is your time to rise.

Right now, take a deep inhale. Hold it. Feel it.

Now exhale. Release. Let go.

This is how you change the storm.

This is how you disengage from Trouble and engage in life.

Now, breathe and throw that S.H.I.T. overboard!

Practical Tools for Release

Breathwork: Inhale peace, exhale Trouble. Use the breath as a tool to reset the nervous system and create space for clarity.

Journaling: Write down the sources of Trouble in your life and see if you can trace them back to decisions you made out of Shame, Hurt or Insecurity. How might you take a different direction in the future when faced with the same decisions?

Affirmations: Declare over and over: "I am not defined by Trouble. I am anchored in peace."

Community: Lean into relationships that ground you, offering a safe harbor in the storms of Trouble.

Visualization: Close your eyes and imagine carrying a cargo box marked "Trouble" and throwing it overboard. What does it feel like to let it go?

Music for Reflection

"Rest" by Lauren McLeod Carter

Chapter Five

DESCENDING INTO THE BELLY OF THE SHIP

The Ship of Souls (Visions during Breathwork sessions)

In the space between breath and vision, where the veil of reality thins, I found myself aboard an ancient vessel—the Ship of Souls. But this wasn't a ship in the way we understand ships. It didn't sail on water. It moved through time itself, carrying the weight of untold stories, the echoes of the forgotten, and the silent screams of generations past.

The air was thick—suffocating with history—a layered mix of brine, sweat, and something deeper, something unshakable. The wooden planks beneath me had been worn smooth by countless footsteps, each one carrying its own burden of hope and heartbreak. As I moved deeper, the atmosphere pressed against my skin, heavy with the unspoken truths of those who had walked this path before me.

This was no mere ship—it was a living archive of human endurance. Every creak in the wood, every gust of air that slipped through its bones carried whispers of love, loss, resistance, and survival.

Then came the smell—sharp, layered, impossible to ignore. The bite of rusted iron from chains that once bound wrists and ankles. The damp musk of wood aged by salt and storms. And beneath it all, something more gut-wrenching—the acrid stench of fear, the sickly sweetness of despair, and a stubborn, unyielding scent of hope that refused to be snuffed out.

I descended further into the ship's belly, and the air grew thicker, pressing against me like a force determined to pull me under. This was where human cargo had been packed, shoulder to shoulder, breath to breath. The silence wasn't really silent—it was a roaring quiet, a storm of grief and rage locked inside the walls. A heavy chorus of silent screams and whispered prayers, echoes of sorrow too deep to fade.

Rusted chains lay scattered on the floor—not just relics of suffering, but proof of survival. If the walls could talk, they'd tell of secret handholds in the dark, fingers clasped together in defiance, songs of freedom hummed beneath the weight of oppression. Even in bondage, the spirit refused to die.

The weight of it settled over me, and then—Aaksum's voice. Steady. Strong. An anchor in the storm.

"This is your lineage," Aaksum said. "But it does not define you. It is both your burden and your gift."

The fire in my chest wasn't just my own rage—it was ancestral rage, passed down in the blood, imprinted on the soul. The confusion, the disorientation—it wasn't just mine. It was the echo of displacement, the uprooting, the casting away. Yet through all of it, there was a clear call—a knowing, a responsibility that stretched beyond time.

I saw myself as I am now at the bottom of the ship, looking at enslaved people—some standing, some collapsed in a pile of lifeless bodies. I panicked. The vision felt too raw, too much—so I left it.

But the reason I was doing the breathwork was to gain clarity for the book you hold in your hand—Shipwreck: Throw That S.H.I.T. Overboard. I knew I had to go back.

So, I did the breathwork again.

This time, I was ready to face it.

A being—Aaksum—stood before me.

"This is your lineage," they said, "but do not take from it bitterness, hatred, or unforgiveness. If you keep repeating history, the Earth will not heal. Hurt people hurt people. BE HEALED."

Their words hit me deep. The weight of history was suffocating, but they weren't asking me to carry it the way I thought.

I was angry—fuming, actually. Disappointed to the bone. I wanted justice, fire, retribution. But somehow, love and forgiveness kept rising higher than my rage. Eclipsing it. Not erasing it, but dimming its control.

I couldn't wrap my head around it. How could they forgive like this? How could they stand in the ruins and still offer grace?

"Their experience was painful," Aaksum said, "and they do not want it repeated."

Then, they placed me in a white sheet atop the dead bodies. Two beings stood beside me, also in white, forming a glowing triangle at the bottom of the ship. The forgiveness that washed over me was overwhelming—otherworldly.

Then came the final test.

"Dive in," they said.

I looked around, searching for some sign of what they meant. The ship still felt solid beneath my feet, the air thick with the weight of memory. The bodies below me, the echoes of the past clinging to the walls—was I supposed to dive into that? Into history itself? Into the suffering they had endured?

I hesitated, my mind racing. Dive where? I had no idea. My breath caught as I realized that this wasn't about physically moving—this was about surrender. About stepping into the unknown, releasing my fear, and trusting that I wouldn't drown in what came next.

Aaksum spoke again: "We are not here, and neither are we angry."

Confused, I asked, "Where are you? And why aren't you angry?"

If they weren't here, then where were they? And more importantly—why was I here? Had they brought me? Had I stumbled upon this place by accident, or had I been called?

A thousand questions swirled in my mind, my pulse quickening. If you've transcended, then why am I standing in the belly of this ship, feeling every ounce of the pain that was left behind? Did you bring me here? And for what?

The air around me felt charged, like the moment before a storm, heavy with something unseen. Aaksum's presence remained steady, unmoving. Their expression held neither sadness nor regret—only clarity.

Aaksum's expression was steady, full of something deeper than peace—understanding.

"Because we have transcended. Anger is a weight we were never meant to carry forever. Our suffering was real, but we do not live there anymore. If you keep holding onto anger, you are not honoring us—you are chaining yourself to what we endured. We want you to be free."

The air shifted, and suddenly, the ship transformed. The dark, musty hold of suffering faded into golden light, spilling over an endless field of sunflowers.

Aaksum gestured toward the sea of golden blooms. "Look closely," they said. "The sunflower is not what it seems. What you think are petals are actually leaves, disguising themselves in golden brilliance to attract life. And the center? The dark, seeded part? That is where the true flowers bloom—hundreds, thousands of them, in perfect alignment, creating something greater than themselves."

I watched as the wind moved through the field, carrying whispers of stories, healing, and something so much bigger than me.

"You see, healing is not on the surface—it happens within. The oppressed and the oppressor have been tangled in darkness for too long. But here, in the center, they are together—not in chains, but in unity. That is the truth of the sunflower, the truth of healing. It is not about forgetting. It is about transforming."

Aaksum's voice softened, but the words struck deep. "Will you carry the pain? Or will you bloom?"

Suddenly, the vision shifted. The ship dissolved, and I saw both the oppressed and the oppressor standing together. The darkness gave way to something entirely new—a sunflower.

At the center of that sunflower—the dark, seeded part—the oppressed and the oppressors stood together, loving one another, embraced in unity. And around them? A vast field of sunflowers, stretching endlessly, swaying in the Son's sunlight.

* * *

Belonging is one of the most basic human needs. We are wired to connect, to find our place within a community, to feel seen, understood, and valued. But often, our wounds dictate where and how we seek that belonging. They tether us to groups and identities that reinforce our pain, binding us to stories born out of our past experiences. There's a certain allure—a sense of empowerment—that comes from belonging, even if it's to a toxic group or ideology. Once you identify with something, you're hooked. That identification becomes a lifeline, a badge of honor, or even a shield, protecting you from the discomfort of standing alone.

This dynamic is trauma bonding at its core. Trauma bonds are formed when pain becomes the glue that holds us to people, groups, or narratives, even when they harm us. It's a paradoxical relationship: the very thing that perpetuates our suffering also gives us a sense of security and identity. We cling to it because it's familiar, even comforting in its toxicity. These bonds whisper, *"At least here, I know my place. At least here, my pain is understood."* But this kind of belonging is not a true connection—it's survival. It's a way to avoid the discomfort of breaking free, even when freedom is what we need most.

This is the trap of pride and insecurity—they are two sides of the pendulum, both seeking the same outcome: a sense of belonging and identity. Pride says, *"I'm better than them; I belong because of my superiority."* Insecurity whispers, *"I'm not enough, so I'll attach myself to this group or cause to feel whole."* Both are rooted in the same fundamental desire: to matter, to have a place, to be someone. Trauma bonds intensify this desire, convincing us that without these toxic attachments, we'll lose our sense of self altogether.

But here's the critical question: What story or narrative are you buying into to feel this sense of belonging? Is it a story that lifts you, or one that keeps you small? Is it a narrative rooted in truth, or one steeped in fear, division, and limitation? And what, exactly, are you fighting for? Are you fighting for healing, wholeness, and unity? Or are you fighting to defend a story that no longer serves you—a story that perpetuates your pain because it feels safer than confronting the unknown?

Slavery wasn't just an act of dehumanization—it created a trauma bond that still lingers today, binding us together through shared pain instead of healing. This generational wound, rooted in exploitation, separation, and survival at any cost, has evolved into a modern-day prison of offense, fear, and unforgiveness. This keeps us locked in a cycle of pain, anger, and identity tied to suffering, making it hard to break free. It convinces us that letting go of pain means forgetting injustice, when in reality, healing is not erasure—it's liberation.

But this trauma is more than an emotional or mental problem—it's physical, too. Our bodies hold the pain of our ancestors, manifesting as phantom pains, chronic tension, and exhaustion—as if history is written into our very bones.

Scripture warns us about this self-perpetuating cycle. Hebrews 3:12 (NLT) says, "Be careful then, dear brothers and sisters. Make sure that your own hearts are not evil and unbelieving, turning you away from the living God." Staying tied to offense and unforgiveness keeps us from trusting in God's sovereignty, justice, and provision. This mindset of scarcity and separation makes true reconciliation seem impossible.

Jesus breaks it down even further in Matthew 7:3-5 (NIV), when He says, "Why do you look at the speck of sawdust in your brother's eye and pay no attention to the plank in your own eye?" This trauma bond makes us hyper-aware of injustice, privilege, and wrongdoing in others, while ignoring the unforgiveness, fear, and unbelief weighing down our own hearts. But freedom doesn't come from keeping score—it comes from surrender.

Slavery's trauma bond thrives because it reinforces the lie of separation. Yet, 1 Corinthians 12:12 (NLT) reminds us: "The human body has many parts, but the many parts make up one whole body. So it is with the body of Christ." We are not enemies. We are not competitors fighting over scraps. We are one body. Breaking free means rejecting division and stepping into unity.

In Matthew 26:11 (NIV), Jesus says: "The poor you will always have with you, but you will not always have me." Poverty—whether material or spiritual—is a byproduct of the scarcity mindset. As long as we cling to offense and division, we will remain impoverished in love, trust, and unity. But Christ calls us into His abundance, where healing isn't just possible—it's promised.

And then, there's God's personal response to my own questioning: "What am I here for?"

His answer? *You are here to love and to be loved. You, Carmen, love like no other on the earth.*

That truth changed everything.

Love—the kind described in 1 Corinthians 13 (NIV), the kind that "keeps no record of wrongs"—is the key to breaking the trauma bond of slavery. Love dismantles division. Love unlocks forgiveness. Love sets both the spirit and the body free from the weight of anger, fear, and generational pain.

The Trap of Offense

Matthew 24:10 (NKJV) states, "And then many will be offended, will betray one another, and will hate one another." To be offended is a symptom of unbelief. Let's define the word offense:

Transliteration: skandalon

Phonetic Spelling: (skan'-dal-on)

Definition: A stick for bait (of a trap), generally a snare, a stumbling block, an offense.

When we are spiritually immature, offenses take root and linger, feeding cycles of resentment and pain. Offense is a symptom of unbelief, revealing where we have chosen not to trust God's sovereignty, justice, or design. It is a stumbling block, a trap that keeps us ensnared in cycles of bitterness and division.

This truth resonates deeply in the context of race and culture, where offense has often shaped our decisions and identities. As a Black woman, I choose not to carry offense over the legacy of slavery, recognizing that doing so only perpetuates division and insecurity in myself and others. Instead, I acknowledge that even when I question God—about privilege, injustice, or anything else—my response to unanswered questions determines whether I walk in faith or remain trapped in anger.

Holding onto offense, anger, or the pain of the past doesn't just weigh on our spirits—it wreaks havoc on our bodies. Dr. Bessel van der Kolk states in *The Body Keeps the Score,* "Our bodies store the impact of trauma, carrying unresolved emotional pain in ways we may not even realize, storing unresolved emotional pain as physical symptoms."[5] If we choose to hold onto the wounds of slavery, the members of our own body bear the burden. Phantom pains—aches in the shoulders, legs, or back—begin to manifest as the body processes the emotional weight we refuse to release. This decision, rooted in fear, creates a cycle of suffering within ourselves. It is as though our refusal to let go of offense keeps us imprisoned in a story of pain, with our bodies acting as unwilling participants in the battle.

But love offers a better way. Love teaches us to see ourselves and others as members of one body, uniquely created and equally valued. It calls us to patience and kindness, urging us to approach racial and cultural differences with grace instead of judgment. Love challenges us to release past hurts and walk in forgiveness and reconciliation rather than bitterness and anger.

Love also humbles us, exposing our biases and reminding us that no one is superior or inferior in God's eyes. And love strengthens us, always protecting, trusting, hoping, and persevering as we confront and heal the pain within ourselves. Imagine what the world would look like if we chose to hold no record of wrongs. Without the weight of offense, fear, or anger,

---

5 Bessel van der Kolk, *The Body Keeps the Score: Brain, Mind, and Body in the Healing of Trauma,* (New York: Penguin Books, 2014).

we would walk in freedom, unburdened by the past. Our bodies, freed from the stress and tension of unresolved pain, could heal and thrive. Our communities could reflect God's love, unified in purpose and harmony.

When we choose love, we align our decisions with God's will, allowing healing to flow within and through us. Offense may tempt us to hold onto pain, but faith calls us to trust God, even in the unanswered questions. By choosing love over offense, we not only break the cycle of division but also liberate our bodies and spirits from the burdens of the past. In doing so, we embrace the redemptive power of grace and create a legacy of healing, reconciliation, and unity for generations to come.

The Power of Choosing Healing

Sometimes, we just need to pause. Take a holy breath. And whisper a quiet, "Thank You."

Because here's the truth—our ancestors endured some hardship. Hardship we can't even begin to wrap our minds around. They endured. They survived what should've taken them out. But here's the thing, survival isn't the same as healing. Just because they kept going doesn't mean we're supposed to keep dragging the same pain. Their battles were real—no shade there. But they're not ours to keep fighting. Their souls have moved on. But some of that pain? It lingers. It clings. But only if we keep holding it.

Let me hit you with something simple: Think about it—when leaves fall, the tree doesn't bend over to pick them back up. Why?

Because they served their purpose.
Because they're not meant to be reattached.
Because that season is over.

Some of us are walking around clutching *dead emotional leaves* like they still belong on our branches. Let it drop. Let it rot. Let it feed your roots instead of draining your fruit.

Now, the Word? It's clear about how pain passes on: "I, the Lord your God, am a jealous God, visiting the iniquity of the fathers upon the children to the third and fourth generations of those who hate Me" (Exodus 20:5, NKJV). But don't stop reading there: "...But showing mercy to thousands, to those who love Me and keep My commandments" (Exodus 20:6, NKJV).

"Know therefore that the Lord your God is God... keeping His covenant of love to a thousand generations of those who love Him and keep His commandments" (Deuteronomy 7:9, NIV). Look—sin runs for four generations. But mercy? Mercy runs a thousand deep. Sin might have momentum. But mercy has multiplication. And here's where science and Spirit link arms, the study of epigenetics says trauma doesn't just disappear. It travels. It buries itself in our biology. Passed down through the bloodline like a secret nobody talks about. But guess what? Healing can be inherited too. You don't have to carry what they couldn't lay down.

You don't have to bleed for what they never got to grieve. You don't have to become the version of yourself that only knows how to survive. You get to choose something better. "I confess the sins we Israelites, including myself and my father's family, have committed against you" (Nehemiah 1:6, NIV). "Because of our sins and the iniquities of our ancestors..." (Daniel 9:16, NIV). That's not guilt. That's not Shame. That's generational healing in motion: recognition, repentance, and release.

Now let me ask you this straight up: Whose blood gets the final say? The bloodline of your ancestors—marked by survival, suppression, and silence? *Or the blood of Jesus—marked by redemption, restoration, and chain-breaking in both directions?* Because listen—healing is not a mood. It's a move.

You want to break the cycle? You better do more than wish it. You choose it. You move with it. You breathe through it. You act like it. Because when we choose to heal, we don't just heal ourselves. We heal backward. We heal forward. We heal beyond what we can see. But if we don't? We don't stay bound by curses. We stay stuck by choice.

* * *

Music for Meditation

"When God Says Move" by Carmen Calhoun

Chapter Six

Navigating to New Waters

Now that we've spent some time examining the S.H.I.T. we've been hauling around and its potential to wreak havoc in our lives, let's shift our attention to the healing process.

How exactly do we heal? Healing is not a one-time event, not a grand finale where all wounds magically disappear. It is a journey, a lifelong unfolding, a continuous invitation to love yourself where you are while embracing the love of God as you release. There is timing to healing. It is not forced, not rushed, not dictated by the world's demands.

Healing requires trust. Trust is not about control—it's about connection. It's not a power struggle, not a game of dominance and submission. Trust is a divine dance—a rhythm, a giving and receiving, moving in sync, adjusting to the flow of another without losing yourself in the process.

When two people dance, there is no force—only attunement. Each step, each movement, is a conversation. One leads, but not with pressure; the other follows, but not without presence. Both are listening. Both are responding. There is a silent agreement: *I will honor your space, and you will honor mine. I will guide with intention, and you will respond with trust.*

Listening to My Body: A Pathway to Healing

As a Black woman in America, I can honestly say that my decisions have hindered me far more than the color of my skin ever has. It's not systemic racism or external barriers that have defined my path—it's been the choices I've made without considering their long-term consequences. For much of my life, I focused on immediate gratification, making decisions that satisfied the moment but failed to account for the ripple effects they would create five, ten, or even twenty years down the road.

I made those decisions without ever consulting the members of my body, where my trauma, anger, sadness, and bitterness were stored. I wasn't taught—nor did I take the time to educate myself—about how the choices I made would manifest physically, emotionally, and spiritually. One of the most profound examples of this was my decision to have abortions. At the time, I wasn't aware of the weight those choices would carry, not only in my heart but in my entire being. The impact wasn't just emotional—it was physical, affecting everything from my feet to the crown of my head, and everything in between.

The trauma I carried didn't remain abstract; it lived in my body, influencing how I moved through the world. My feet ached under the weight of unfulfilled potential, my stomach churned with regret, and my shoulders bore the heaviness of shame I didn't even realize I was holding. These choices weren't made in isolation, and neither were their effects. They were compounded by the lack of awareness, education, and introspection that might have helped me make more informed, intentional decisions.

The truth is, my body was trying to communicate with me all along. It stored the unprocessed emotions, the sadness, and the anger I never addressed. But I ignored those signals, choosing instead to live in a state of detachment from myself. It wasn't until much later that I began to understand how these decisions shaped my life—not because of external forces or societal oppression, but because I had never truly learned how to listen to myself, how to heal, or how to honor my own body and spirit.

*   *   *

Getting back behind the wheel of my dump truck in the summer of 2024 felt like reclaiming a piece of myself. After time away, I was ready—eager even—to haul loads, navigate long hours, and fall back into the familiar rhythm of work. At first, it felt empowering. I had missed the hum of the engine, the steady rumble of the road beneath me. But it wasn't long before something else made its presence known—pain.

It started as a minor twinge in my right shoulder, easy to ignore. But day by day, it escalated. The constant steering, shifting gears, and truck vibrations aggravated it, spreading the ache down my arm, numbing my fingers, climbing into my neck and upper back. By the end of each day, my shoulder felt locked, frozen, damn near useless.

Simple tasks became mini battles. Reaching for a water bottle? Jolt of pain. Adjusting the mirrors? Another shockwave. Sleeping? Forget about it. Every position hurt. Mornings were stiff and miserable—I had to shake my legs just to get moving. Frustration seeped into my prayers. "God, if we're under a better covenant than Moses, why is my body acting like this? I'm only in my 50s!" My once-strong, reliable body felt like it was betraying me. And I was angry.

Desperation led me to a chiropractor. After a thorough evaluation, she barely hesitated before saying, "Your C7 is out of alignment. And your hips? They're screaming at me."

I blinked. *My hips?* I hadn't even considered that. But as she explained how my body had been compensating for misalignment, it clicked—the shoulder pain wasn't the root issue. It was a symptom. The adjustments were brutal. When she worked on my hips, the pain was sharp, overwhelming. Tears streamed down my face as she pressed and pulled, realigning areas that had been out of place for way too long. Then came my spine—specifically, C7. One firm adjustment, and it felt like something locked deep inside me had finally been set free.

I left the session physically sore but spiritually shaken. Something had shifted. Before I walked out, the chiropractor hit me with a hard truth: "You have to change your thinking, or you'll end up out of alignment again."

Her words wouldn't leave me. My body wasn't some machine to be fixed. My thoughts, emotions, and physical body were all connected. If I didn't address the patterns that put me here, no amount of realignment would keep me healed.

I had work to do—inside and out.

Healing: Deeper Relief – The Stretch Therapist

Even after the chiropractor's adjustments, my shoulder still felt tight—like something was refusing to let go. A friend recommended a stretch therapist, so I figured, why not? The chiropractor had been all about forceful realignment, but this? This was different. The stretch therapist's movements were slow, deliberate, and calming, almost like she was coaxing my body into trusting her.

During my first session, she ran her hands along my body, scanning for tension. When she reached my legs, she paused. "Your right quad is elevated. It's compensating for something else. We've got to figure that out." I hadn't noticed anything wrong with my leg—until she said it. Then, suddenly, I could feel it. It was as if my body had been silently screaming for help, waiting for someone to actually listen.

She had me relax completely. As she supported my arm, I realized just how much tension I had been unconsciously holding. When she started working on the fascia near my shoulder, gently squeezing the tissue under my armpit, I felt something shift. A lightness. A release.

Then she moved deeper. She lifted my arm over my head and, using her forearm, pressed along my rib cage toward my armpit. I had spent so much energy holding myself together that I hadn't even noticed how much effort I put into simply existing. And then she hit a spot that made me want to fly off the table.

"What the hell is that?" I yelped.

She smiled knowingly. "That's your fascia—years of tension stored up."

As she worked, something unexpected happened—memories surfaced. Out of nowhere, I saw a moment from high school: a classmate slapping me across the face. I couldn't even remember why, but the sting of that slap had lived inside me for over thirty years.

It wasn't only about that slap. It was about every slap— physical, emotional, verbal—I had ever taken. Resentment, anger, disappointment—they had all buried themselves deep in my body, stored in places I never thought to check.

Then, Matthew 18:21-22 (NKJV) came to mind: "'Lord, how many times will my brother sin against me, and I forgive him? Up to seven times?' Jesus answered him, 'I say to you, not up to seven times, but seventy times seven.'"

Peter was me. *How many times do I have to forgive, Lord? Because I'm tired.* But it's not about keeping count. It's about letting go—again and again—until it no longer owns you. With every press of her hands, I made a choice. I forgave the classmate.

I forgave myself for holding onto it for so long. I forgave the moments that had shaped me in ways I didn't even realize.

Each act of forgiveness felt like peeling back layers of tension—layers I didn't even know were there. And as I let go, my body let go, too.

At one point, the therapist stopped and said, "I did that intuitively. I've never done it before." Her words stopped me in my tracks. She wasn't following a standard technique. She was responding to what my body needed at that moment. That's when I realized—healing isn't a formula. It's a conversation. A relationship between body, mind, and spirit.

By the end of the session, I wasn't only stretched—I was lighter. Not just physically, but emotionally and spiritually too. The weight I had been carrying for decades had finally started to lift. And for the first time in a long time, I felt free.

A Journey Toward Wholeness

The pain I had been carrying was more than a physical issue. It was a manifestation of unprocessed emotions and unacknowledged burdens. The chiropractor had shown me the importance of realignment, even when it's painful. The stretch therapist taught me the value of gentleness, intuition, and listening to my body. Together, they helped me see that healing isn't just about fixing what's broken—it's about addressing the root causes, honoring the body's messages, and letting go of what no longer serves me.

Driving my truck again may have reignited the pain, but it also led me to a deeper understanding of myself. Healing isn't a destination; it's a journey of awareness, patience, and forgiveness. As I move forward, I carry these lessons with me, trusting my body's wisdom and embracing the process of becoming whole.

* * *

Music for Meditation

"Awesome God The Dump Truck Song"
by Carmen Calhoun

Chapter Seven

SET YOUR RADAR TO RECEIVE

True generosity is a beautiful quality, but somewhere along the way, we learned to give for the wrong reasons. Most of us were taught that giving—whether to a church, a charity, or society's endless demands—is something you're obligated to do. No questions asked. But when giving comes from guilt or pressure, it leaves you drained, resentful, and feeling like you're pouring into a cup with no bottom.

Giving was never meant to deplete you. Giving should flow from a place of abundance and gratitude. It starts with receiving, celebrating what you have, and then sharing from the overflow. That's the design: You care for yourself and your family first, and from that foundation, love and generosity can flow outward. It's not selfish—it's smart. It's how you make a real impact without losing yourself in the process.

We've got to shift our mindset, realigning ourselves with the principles God designed for our lives. And no, this isn't about some abstract, unreachable standard. It's about getting back to basics, letting go of the S.H.I.T. weighing us down, and stepping into practices that actually turn the tide toward freedom.

Romans 5:17 (NKJV) says, "...much more those who receive abundance of grace and of the gift of righteousness will reign in life through the One, Jesus Christ." So let me ask you this: If you're not reigning in your life, could it be that you've got a receiver problem? Here's the good news—it's an easy fix. RECEIVE!

First up: faithful receiving. Listen, I know this might sound radical, but the world has conditioned us to resist what's already ours. Even receiving feels unnatural—like a battle between worthiness and hesitation. That little voice whispering, *Do you really deserve this?* Silence it. Yes, you do. And here's another one: *Oh, you didn't have to do that for me.* Really? As if you had insider knowledge of what God instructed someone to do on your behalf.

Receiving isn't selfish; it's alignment. It's stepping into the flow of grace already in motion. In fact, it's worship—because when you receive it fully, you affirm God's goodness and allow His work to be completed in you. That's the very thing that fueled Jesus after freeing the Samaritan woman. While the disciples were focused on physical food, Jesus was already full—sustained by the act of breaking chains, restoring dignity, and unleashing a woman into the freedom she never knew she could claim. His satisfaction came from doing the Father's will, and guess what? Yours does too. So take the blessing. Take the grace. Walk in the overflow. That's how you honor the gift.

Many have been led to believe that it pleases God for us to be broke, downtrodden, and struggling—as if suffering itself is some kind of spiritual badge of honor. But let's set the record straight: God is not glorified in our lack; He is glorified in our liberation. Yes, there is purpose in pain, and yes, trials refine us, but being perpetually bound by scarcity—whether financial, emotional, or spiritual—is not the mark of divine favor. Jesus didn't come so we could scrape by in misery; He came to give "life more abundantly" (John 10:10, NKJV).

When Jesus freed the Samaritan woman, He didn't leave her broken at the well—He empowered her, restored her, and sent her forward overflowing with testimony. Your thriving is not a problem for God; it's His pleasure. It's time to stop equating holiness with hardship and start receiving the fullness of what He's already made available. Freedom honors Him. Thriving in His abundance—whatever that looks like for you—is a testimony of His goodness, not a betrayal of it.

Here's the truth: God didn't call you to just survive; He called you to reign. And if you're going to reign, it starts with being open to receive—grace, blessings, and yes, the good stuff He's got lined up just for you. This is how you step into the life you're designed to live, not by over-giving, not by running on empty, but by faithfully receiving and letting that overflow bless others.

Thoughtful Giving: A Heart Aligned with God's Principles

You know what? Giving isn't supposed to feel like you're a contestant on Survivor, sacrificing your last piece of bread to win approval from an imaginary jury. It's not a game, and it's definitely not about making yourself miserable to prove you're holy or generous enough. Seriously, who started that rumor? Probably the same person who thought kale chips could replace Doritos.

Think about it: Your giving should feel like planting seeds in fertile soil, knowing they'll grow into something meaningful— not tossing those seeds into a black hole where nothing ever comes back. You're not a human ATM. Thoughtful giving is more than generosity; it's about trusting God's provision, aligning with His principles, and letting your heart guide your hand.

Let's take a moment to talk about the poor widow in Mark 12:41-44. She gave two mites—all she had—and Jesus praised her. Not because she was broke and still gave, but because of her heart. She wasn't showing off or giving out of guilt. She gave with faith and trust in God, while others gave from their excess without sacrifice. Here's the catch, though: Her story also shines a spotlight on the broken systems that left her destitute in the first place. Systems that should've lifted her up but failed her. *What-in-the-John-Brown kind of setup is that?*

Not everyone goes to church, and that's just reality. But here's the wild part—most who do (around two-thirds, depending on the study) show up not necessarily out of deep devotion, but out of fear, guilt, or a sense of obligation. They've been conditioned to believe they need to "pay up"—whether through tithes, offerings, or just showing face—to keep the Big Man (God) off their back. It's almost like a divine tax, a way to dodge some kind of cosmic consequence.

Now, let's unpack something Jesus said that's always been a head-scratcher for me: "The poor you will always have with you" (Matthew 26:11, NIV). What? Doesn't that sound like it's clashing with His other statement, "I came to give you life and life more abundantly" (John 10:10, NKJV)? It's like, which is it, Jesus? But hold up—it's not a contradiction. It's about choice and free will. God's abundance is always there, but He's not going to force you to take it. It's like a buffet—you can pile your plate high or sit there starving while everyone else eats. Your call.

And speaking of missing out, my dad used to drop this gem: "If you want to hide something from a Black person, put it in a book, Sugarbabe." Now, before you start gasping, clutching pearls, or drafting a think-piece, let's be clear—this isn't just about Black folks; it's about everybody. I've bought countless books for people of all backgrounds—Asian, White, Latino, you name it—and guess what? They still haven't read them. Turns out, unread books are a universal struggle.

We get distracted, we *mean* to get around to it, and before we know it, the book is collecting dust while we binge another show. If knowledge is power, then a whole lot of folks are out here voluntarily unarmed. Provision and wisdom have been hiding in plain sight for centuries—whether in books, teachings, or divine whispers. But instead of opening the pages, people reject truth just because it doesn't fit their belief system. It's like God's handing out treasure maps, and we're too busy saying, "Nah, I'm good," while holding a McDonald's receipt.

Let me tell you about my treasure moment. It was 11:35 pm, and I was minding my own business when the Holy Spirit whispered, *Hey, go invest in that token.* Now, I didn't know the first thing about crypto (I do now), but when the Holy Spirit speaks, you listen. So I threw in $100 and went to bed. When I woke up the next morning, my account was at $800. What?! Honey, I was drunk on the love of God for that blessing.

But here's the thing—when God blesses you like that, it's not just about keeping it to yourself. Oh no. I wasn't just ready to give; I wanted to *teach.* Why? Because what good is giving a fish when you can teach someone to fish—or in this case, how to hear the Holy Spirit whispering financial advice? That's the real overflow—blessing others in a way that empowers them to thrive, not just survive.

When your cup is full—literally and metaphorically—you're not just surviving, you're thriving. You're walking around with that tipsy-on-love vibe, seeing the world through the lens of abundance. And from that place? Oh, honey, you can give in ways that empower, restore, and uplift others—without burning yourself out. So grab your blessing and then share the overflow in a way that teaches others how to thrive, too.

Investing for Multiplication

Make an offering of ten percent, a tithe, of all the produce which grows in your fields year after year. Bring this into the

Presence of God, your God, at the place he designates for worship and there eat the tithe from your grain, wine, and oil and the firstborn from your herds and flocks. In this way you will learn to live in deep reverence before God, your God, as long as you live. But if the place God, your God, designates for worship is too far away and you can't carry your tithe that far, God, your God, will still bless you: Exchange your tithe for money and take the money to the place God, your God, has chosen to be worshiped. Use the money to buy anything you want: cattle, sheep, wine, or beer—anything that looks good to you. You and your family can then feast in the Presence of God, your God, and have a good time. Deuteronomy 14: 22-26 (MSG)

Growing up, I thought that giving money to God was a duty and a protection from bad things happening. It wasn't until I began studying Deuteronomy 14 that I realized I had been seeing things upside down. God's design for giving flips this whole mess we've been believing right on its head. His plan is refreshingly simple and, honestly, kind of fun. It starts with receiving first—taking care of yourself and your family, celebrating His provision with joy, and yes, let's not skip the wine and beer. That's right, God said it Himself. You need the wine! Because, let's be honest, a good glass of wine makes you a little tipsy, a little lighter, and sometimes even delightfully delusional. And baby, the love of God? It has exactly the same effect—but it's calorie-free and lasts forever. *Shundala!*

Most of us have no idea about the true meaning of the tithe, or that God's design for abundance isn't about just scraping by or barely making ends meet—it's about overflow, baby. Overflow! We're talking about divine abundance that makes you sit up and go, *Wait, is this my life?* And it's not confined to a church pew or some guilt-driven collection plate. Nope, the "place he designates for worship" is like a high-performance vehicle—a carrier for your seed that's designed to multiply, not just maintain. Oh, the places you will go (thank you, Dr. Seuss)! Whether it's crypto, stocks, commodities, a ministry, or that big dream you've been too scared to act on, the magic happens when you plant your seed exactly where God directs.

Let's break it down. The "place he designates for worship" isn't just a catchy phrase—Deuteronomy 14 says, "Then *eat the tithe* from your grain, wine, and oil and the firstborn from your herds and flocks." (Pause for effect, and now sing it in the tune of Michael Jackson's *Beat It*— "Just Eat it, Eat it"—you're welcome.) Did you catch that? God didn't say, "Tithe and walk away." No, Sugar. He said, "Eat before the Lord!" Translation: Celebrate His provision with joy, gratitude, and yes, let's not forget the wine and beer because it's right there in scripture! You know what that means? This isn't some boring, guilt-driven ritual; it's a full-blown worship party! (Looks like God was showing us the Holy Communion, the grain [the bread] and the wine [the blood].) So grab a plate, pour a drink, and toast to His goodness—because God didn't come to give you rules, He came to give you life!

And here's where it gets real—this isn't just about you. And before anyone gets it twisted, let me be clear: I am *not* against giving to your church. If you belong to a local church where you receive the Word of God and worship, you should absolutely give, sow seed, and support it. Like any organization, churches need funding—to keep the doors open, serve the community, and carry out the mission God has given them.

But here's the bigger picture—God's flow of giving isn't limited to one place. Sugar, let God—aka Daddy—get His worship on too! He *delights* in you enjoying His provision, His abundance,

His gifts. It's part of how He gets glory—by watching His kids dance in what He freely gives. This is a circle dance, honey, a real flow. You receive, celebrate, and give back—all designed to bless not just you but all the nations of the earth. When you invest where He leads—whether it's a ministry, a business, or that bold creative dream—you're stepping into a flow that multiplies blessings like nobody's business. It's not about obligation; it's about obedience and overflow.

And speaking of overflow, let's talk about spiritual multiplication. Honey, this is kingdom gardening with a sprinkle of divine franchising. When you sow into churches, ministries, or faith-driven missions, you're not just dropping a dollar in a bucket—you're planting seeds that grow faith, transform lives, and spread God's truth (spiritually speaking). It's like throwing heavenly fertilizer on the soil of eternity. And that crop? Let's just say, we're believing for a divine return.

God's abundance doesn't ride a tricycle—it's got a turbocharged engine and a GPS straight to overflow. This is where you take that seed and invest it in businesses, creative projects, or in the stock market. I had a Bible-thumper once ask me, "You really think God would tell you to invest in the stock market? That's not in the Bible." And you know what I told them? "Neither is driving that Lincoln Navigator you're flexing in, but you sure didn't mind writing that check, did you?"

This is what's wrong with a lot of religious folks today—they don't evolve, they don't innovate. They stay stuck, thinking "God doesn't change" means He's parked on some heavenly rocking chair, stiff, aching, and handing out orders like it's 1895.

Newsflash: God changes not—yeah, that's Malachi 3:6 (NIV): "I the LORD do not change. So you, the descendants of Jacob, are not destroyed." But that doesn't mean He's stagnant.

God is ever moving, ever innovating, ever creating! He's the same in character, in faithfulness, in love—but His strategies? His methods? His flow? Oh, honey, He's always ahead of the curve.

Imagine God saying, *I see your vision, and I'm ready to take it from zero to a hundred real quick.* It's like divine venture capitalism, where every idea aligned with His purpose becomes an opportunity for exponential growth. Whether you're buying crypto, flipping real estate, or finally launching that gourmet food truck you've been dreaming about, following God's lead breaks the cycle of lack and sets you up with a legacy of abundance.

Here's the beauty of it all: faithful investment—whether spiritual or material—isn't just about building wealth; it's about aligning with God's principles. When you let Him guide where and how you plant your seed (money, time, and talent, but mostly money), the blessings don't just fill your cup—they overflow, creating ripple effects that touch lives you didn't even know you could impact. This is legacy-building. This is kingdom work. This is you, walking in the fullness of God's design for your life.

Kick Scarcity to the Curb

Let's be real: It's easy to give in to fear when it comes to finances. It's the voice in your head—the voice of scarcity. Let's call her *Sally,* the freeloading roommate who refuses to move out. Sally is sprawled out on your mental couch, getting fat on your snacks, whispering, *There's not enough to go around* or *what if you run out?* Meanwhile, you're stress-eating your way through a family-sized bag of worry, thinking, *Sally must be right.* But let's be real—Sally isn't helping. Sally's taking up space, contributing nothing, and leaving crumbs everywhere.

Here's what you're gonna do: Kick that chic out! March up to her with a metaphorical eviction notice and say, "Sally, your time is up. Pack your S.H.I.T., and don't let the door hit you on the way out." Then grab the biggest, boldest bottle of "Changed Mind" air freshener you can find (spicy with a hint of "Vengeance is the Lord's"), and spray that sucker like it's a cleansing ritual.

But don't stop there. Replace Sally's lies with facts and truths. Stand in the middle of your mental living room, take a deep breath and declare: "God's got me. There's more than enough. His blessings aren't on backorder, and I refuse to live in lack anymore!" You're not only evicting Sally but every stinking lie she dragged in with her.

And here's where it gets real good: When Sally's gone, you'll notice how much space she was hogging. Suddenly, there's room for you to dream and manifest, joy to stretch out, for creativity to pop its head up, and for hope to kick its feet up like it belongs there—because it does. Without Sally's mess, you start operating differently. You stop hoarding blessings like they're about to disappear, and you start living like you know who your source is. Spoiler: It's God, and His supply chain is *never* disrupted.

Listen, you don't have time to let Sally steal another day of your peace, your purpose, or your potential. Kick her out, fumigate your mind with truth, and let her know she's been replaced by faith, abundance, and joy. Because you don't just survive—you thrive. You don't just get by—you overflow. And honey, when your blessings start stacking up, Sally's gonna be out there peeking through the window, jealous as hell. Let her watch. *Shundala!*

But just in case Sally tries to sneak back in—rockin' a fake judge's robe and a plastic gavel like she's presiding over a courtroom in your mind—pause and remember this: She's not the Judge! And neither is your S.H.I.T. —your Shame, Hurt, Insecurities, or Trouble.

Because in Malachi 3:5 (NKJV), God doesn't say He's coming to destroy you. He says: "I will come near you for judgment; I will be a swift witness…" That word "judgment" in Hebrew is "mishpat"—not condemnation, but *course correction. Order restoration.* And a witness? A witness doesn't condemn. A witness reveals. A witness testifies: "Here's what's really been robbing you." A judge decides. A witness exposes.

This isn't God raising a gavel to crush you. This is Him holding up a mirror, not to shame you—but to show you the cracks in the flow. So you can get it back. All of it.

See, the poverty mindset? It doesn't just block your finances—it corrupts your view of God, of yourself, and of the divine flow. So God pulls back the curtain—not to shame you, but to free you. And how does He do that?

He reminds you of His original multiplication strategy in Deuteronomy 14:22–28. Let's break it down in modern terms: God said to bring the tithe of your increase—grain, wine, oil, livestock—and EAT IT in His presence. If the distance is too far? Convert it into silver (aka money), travel, and buy whatever your heart desires: livestock, wine, strong drink. Then feast. Rejoice. Circulate the blessing.

This isn't just economic—it's deeply spiritual. This is communion. This is union. This is the rhythm of divine partnership. Because here's the blueprint of heaven's economy:

- Receive the increase (salary, commissions, gifts, dividends, divine deposits).
- Tithe with intention—starting with your household. Speak over it. Say: "This is my seat at the table. This is my declaration of trust."
- Eat the tithe—yes, partake of communion, celebration, and presence. Don't just give—receive.

- Invest in multiplying assets:
    - Real estate (land still multiplies).
    - Stocks and dividends (modern vineyards).
    - Crypto or blockchain (emerging wealth streams).
    - Intellectual property (books, music, courses).
    - Business ownership (today's sheep and cattle).
    - Personal development (when you grow, your world does too).

Give from your overflow. Take care of your family, bless the vulnerable, pour back into the community, and keep that circulation going. Because poverty? It's not just about money. Poverty is not simply the absence of money—it's the presence of lack-based thinking.

When we abandon God's economy, we fall into the mindset that leads to the symptoms listed in Malachi 3:5: manipulation, broken covenant, lies, injustice, exploitation. These are not just sins—they are the social decay that flows from stepping out of divine alignment.

Look at what God names—sorcerers, adulterers, liars, exploiters, and justice-deniers. These aren't random sins; they're symptoms.

- Sorcery? That's manipulation in the absence of trust.
- Adultery? It's breaking covenant—when you no longer believe faithfulness pays off.
- Perjury? That's fear pretending to be wisdom.
- Exploitation? It's hoarding in the name of survival.
- Denying justice to outsiders? That's scarcity turning into suspicion.

They all grow in the soil of poverty thinking. Not just poor in pocket, but poor in trust. Poor in vision. Poor in divine connection. So when Sally tries to come back whispering lies about lack and "never enough," you look her dead in the eye and say: "My tithe is my seat at the table. I don't hoard—I circulate. I don't fear—I invest. I don't survive—I overflow."

Because the judgment in Malachi 3:5? It's not God bringing punishment down from heaven. It's the built-in consequence of stepping out of divine flow. Like gravity—you don't break the law, the law breaks you when you ignore it. So God, in His mercy, becomes a witness. He says, "Look—I'm showing you what's been stealing from you so you can take it all back."

And now let's make it intimate: He says, *You rob Me of watching you enjoy what I gave you. You rob Me of seeing you tipsy with joy, sipping wine over a good meal, blessing your family from overflow, laughing out loud with the people you love, investing in ideas I planted in you, building something that multiplies. I don't just give good gifts—I delight in watching you enjoy them.*

Like any good parent, God delights in your delight. He longs to see you open what He gave you. Not just tithes in a basket, but time at the table. Not just duty. Communion. Not just survival. Circulation. So, the next time Sally tries to slip in with her plastic gavel and whisper you back into fear, guilt, or religious duty? Pull out your blueprint. Remind yourself of the rhythm: Receive. Tithe. Eat. Invest. Circulate. Repeat. Because you were never meant to live outside the flow.

And your God? He's been saving your seat at the table all along.

And now that you see it you'll never eat alone again.

Shundala.

* * *

Music for Meditation

"I Am" by Carmen Calhoun

Chapter Eight

IN THE SAFE HARBOR OF HEALING

The principles I've shared in this book are not abstract for me—they are deeply personal. For years, I carried the story of my molestation as if it were the defining chapter of my life. Those dark years, spanning five to six years of my adolescence, felt like an eternity while I was living them. The trauma shaped my relationships, my self-worth, and even my ability to trust the world around me. But one day, I realized I was living in a loop, replaying the same story over and over, as if my entire existence was written by someone else's actions. I knew I had a choice: to remain bound by that story or to heal and rewrite my narrative.

Healing wasn't immediate. It wasn't linear. It required courage to confront the pain I had buried for so long. I sought therapy to unpack the emotional scars. I turned to somatic bodywork to release the memories stored in my muscles and tissues. And I discovered the transformative power of Breathwork—a practice that taught me how to exhale what no longer served me and inhale the fullness of life, love, and possibility.

This journey taught me that healing is not a destination—it is an ongoing process. I am constantly throwing S.H.I.T. overboard. Every day, I ask myself: *Does this serve me?* If it does, I keep it. If I don't understand it, I set it aside until I do. But if it weighs me down, robs me of joy, or tethers me to a past that no longer belongs to me, I let it go. Sometimes I even laugh as I do it. There's something liberating about declaring, *"Nope, not today!"* and watching that S.H.I.T. sink to the bottom of the ocean.

Healing doesn't mean forgetting. It doesn't mean pretending the pain wasn't real. It means choosing not to let that pain be the centerpiece of your life. It means reclaiming your power and telling a new story. Breathwork taught me this invaluable lesson: every exhale is a release, every inhale an invitation. Life is a rhythm of letting go of what no longer serves you and opening yourself to the abundance God has waiting for you.

There are days when the old story resurfaces, and the pain tries to pull me back into the darkness. But each time, I take a breath and remind myself: *I am not that moment. I am not that pain. I am the woman who survived it, who is healing from it, and who will use it as a stepping stone, not a shackle.*

If you, too, are carrying a painful story, know this: you have the power to heal. You are not your tragedy. You are not your trauma. You are a testament to the resilience of the human spirit. So, when the weight feels unbearable, take a breath, throw that S.H.I.T. overboard, and allow yourself to float in the freedom of grace, healing, and renewal. You are bigger than your pain. You are bigger than your story. You are a reflection of divine strength, and your best chapters are still being written.

The Ruach of God: Breath as the Gateway to Healing

In recent years, I have learned so much about the power of breath. The Hebrew word *ruach* means breath, wind, and spirit. It is the very breath of God—the force of life that animates us, fills us, and sustains our being. The same Ruach that hovered over the waters at creation was the same breath God breathed into Adam, bringing him from dust to life.

We are either creating storms with our breath or taking the wind out of them with the same breath of intention. Breath is more than a function—it is a force. Every inhale has the potential to escalate or de-escalate. Every exhale has the power to release or reinforce.

When we breathe shallow, erratic, and unconscious, we feed the storm. We tell our nervous system that we are in danger, that we must fight, that the storm must rage on. But when we breathe deeply, intentionally, fully, we calm the winds. We tell our minds and our bodies that we are safe, present, and in control.

This is the sacred power of pause. The choice to breathe through instead of lash out. The choice to exhale release instead of inhale more stress. The choice to engage in presence instead of fueling destruction. Breath is more than air moving in and out—it is the gateway between the soul and the body. It is where divine life meets human experience.

You may not be aware of it, but the very life of the triune God is flowing inside your body. The human race was born out of the self-giving love between the Father, Son and Holy Spirit, and Jesus paid the ultimate price to bring us into the center of that love. As Baxter Kruger says, "The gospel is not news of an absent Jesus who waits for us to receive him into our lives. The gospel is the staggering news that Jesus has received us into his life. Jesus has received us into his relationship with his Father, into his anointing with the Spirit, into his relationship with the human race, and into his relationship with the cosmos."[6]

Every inhale is a reminder that God's Spirit still dwells within us; every exhale is a release of what no longer serves us.

The Ruach of God isn't just a poetic metaphor—it's a living, moving force within us. It is the divine reminder that healing is not just an event—it is a practice, a rhythm, a return to Spirit, to God. So when trauma resurfaces, when pain lingers, when the

---

6 Baxter Kruger, "A Note on Jesus Christ and the Church," Perichoresis, June 24, 2020, https://perichoresis.org/a-note-on-jesus-christ-and-the-church/

weight of past wounds tries to keep you stuck, remember this: Breathe. And know that God is still breathing life into you, every moment of every day.

Releasing the Lie

The one thing I knew I was good at was singing. I come from a singing family on my dad's side. I sang in the Glee Club and with the Gospel Choraleers. I won talent shows and traveled around the county performing in my all-red dress. I loved rehearsals—my brother's girlfriend would pick me up, and I never wanted to leave her.

No shade, no judgment—but I don't ever remember anyone from my immediate family showing up to support me in my singing endeavors. When I sang in church, people would yell, "That's Major Gross's daughter!" My dad's family were singers, yet neither he, my mom, nor anyone else ever came to my shows or concerts. No one supported me.

Now, most people know me as a singer, songwriter, and artist. But for years, I created a centrifugal force within my life—a tornado of doubt—where I believed and attracted the lie that my music didn't support me because my experience told me so.

I came to this conclusion after a processing session and Breathwork with my coach and mentor. My intention for the session was clarity and vision in my music career. When she asked what was holding me back, I immediately said, "Money." A belief of lack.

This scarcity mindset started when I was nine years old. I had grown up hearing my parents say, "Money doesn't grow on trees." And alongside that, I experienced their lack of support in my artistic endeavors. I internalized the belief that I couldn't make a living doing what I loved.

That belief showed up in my head and crown area as a weighted, cloudy energy, whispering, *You've done so much work in this area, but it hasn't paid off financially.* Then I thought, *Maybe I need to let go of the financial part.* After all, I have beautiful testimonies of how my music brings others joy. Religion also surfaced during the session, and immediately, a wave of heat rushed from my head to my heart. Shame, Hurt, Insecurities, and Trouble rose to the surface—all waiting to be released.

I sat with Little Carmen and comforted her with words of love and support. Then, we shifted to self-forgiveness. I repeated three or four times: "I forgive myself for buying into the misbelief that I am not supported. The truth is, I am supported. I am loved. I have everything I need pertaining to life and godliness."

We did several rounds of breathing and moving the energy out of my body to facilitate healing. Afterward, the cloud of doubt was gone. It had transformed—white, vibrant, no longer heavy. I felt relief.

The Vision at the Walnut Tree

We followed up the session with Active Breathwork for about 35-40 minutes. As I lay down, I focused on my intention—clarity and vision for my music.

Then, something unexpected happened.

I kept seeing the English walnut tree that stood between my mother's house and my grandmother's house. I climbed it every day as a child. But here, at this moment, I dismissed it—I was looking for clarity, not a tree.

Yet, the tree persisted.

Then, I saw myself hugging the tree—and the visions began. I was visited by my grandmother, aunts, and mother. Now, let me be real—this was freaky. According to my religious beliefs, this should've been an abomination. I couldn't believe what I was experiencing, but then I felt the presence of the Holy Spirit say, *It's okay.*

Then, my grandmother—my mother's mother—whispered, "It's okay."

She repeated it over and over.

Then, my mother's oldest sister appeared. A wave of anger rose in me. I had grown up believing she was responsible for my grandmother's death because she took her out of her home. But Grandma, full of love and compassion, said, "It's okay." And then, to my shock, my mother's oldest sister joined in, repeating the words, "It's okay." Then came my favorite auntie on my mom's side, echoing the same message. And finally—my mother joined them, agreeing.

In all my life, I had never experienced such love, forgiveness, and support—not in my childhood, not in that tree, and not anywhere outside of this vision. They were healing me. They were loving me in ways I hadn't realized I needed. They were showing me that they were a part of my root system—the roots that had been damaged, tangled, and in need of healing.

And they showed up when I was finally ready to receive them.

There was so much forgiveness.

There was so much love.

And for the first time, I felt supported—not just in my music, but in my soul.

This image shows Healing as not a destination, but a living process—a radiant center surrounded by the essential elements that keep it alive. Each circle (Resilience, Empathy, Strength, Recovery, etc.) is not separate from Healing, but an active part of it, like the petals of a flower or the orbiting planets around a sun.

The Molecular Structure of Healing

Image created by Sadia Shahid

In the center, *Healing* shines like the sun—radiating warmth, light, and life outward. The surrounding elements are like planets or satellites, each drawing strength from the center but also giving back energy.

- Without *Connection*, we feel isolated.
- Without *Renewal*, we become stagnant.
- Without *Empathy*, we harden.

Together, these orbiting traits form a solar system of healing, each vital to the whole.

The Circle of Healing Meditation

Close your eyes.
Take a deep breath in… and out.
Feel the ground holding you.
Imagine a glowing circle around you, with healing at its center.
Repeat the following phrases after each bolded word:

Resilience → *I am resilient. I rise again and again.*
Recovery → *I give myself space and time to heal.*
Growth → *I am open to who I am becoming.*
Connection → *I am not alone. I am part of the greater whole.*
Transformation → *I allow myself to evolve.*
Renewal → *Each moment, I am made new.*
Strength → *I am strong, steady, and supported.*
Empathy → *I hold myself with kindness and love.*

Breathe in each quality.
Breathe out anything that no longer serves you.
Return to the center:

I am whole. I am healing. I am exactly where I need to be.

Engage in What Gives Life

Now that we have learned to identify the toxic cargo we've been hauling around, disengage from the storms through the power of breath, and dump limiting beliefs when it comes to receiving abundance, we are ready to make room for what brings us back to life. We can intentionally engage in what revives, restores, and replenishes our mind, body, and soul.

- ✓ **Engage in breathwork**—deep, intentional inhales that flood your system with oxygen and release the stagnant air of yesterday's stress. Let your breath expand your capacity to heal.
- ✓ **Engage in cold showers**—a literal shock to your system that wakes you up, improves circulation, strengthens immunity, and reminds you that discomfort is temporary but growth is lasting.
- ✓ **Engage in real conversations**—not the surface-level, "I'm fine" kind, but the ones that dig deep, uncover the buried wounds, allow vulnerability to replace pretense. Talk to someone who listens.
- ✓ **Engage in movement**—dance, stretch, lift, run, walk, swim. Shake off the stagnancy that has settled in your bones. Move your body like you're shaking off the past, like you're stepping into something new.
- ✓ **Engage in nourishing foods**—not the quick fixes, not the comfort foods that leave you depleted, but the real, whole, living foods that fuel your cells, that sharpen your mind, that remind your body what it means to thrive.

- ✓ **Engage in nature**—let your feet touch the earth, let the sun kiss your skin, let the wind remind you that you are part of something vast and connected. Nature restores what life depletes.
- ✓ **Engage in laughter**—the kind that shakes your ribs, brings tears to your eyes, and reminds you life is meant to be enjoyed, not just endured.
- ✓ **Engage in silence**—not avoidance, but the kind of quiet that lets you hear your own soul, that makes space for divine whispers and deep revelations.
- ✓ **Engage in therapy, counseling, coaching**—whatever support you need to unpack, process, and release what has been weighing you down. Healing doesn't happen in isolation; it happens in safe spaces where we are seen, heard, and understood.
- ✓ **Engage in rest.** Not just sleep, but real, intentional rest—the kind where you lay down the weight of expectation, the hustle, the need to prove something. Rest is resistance in a world that wants you exhausted.
- ✓ **Engage in your dreams.** Pick up that instrument, write that book, start that business, go after that goal. No more waiting. No more postponing yourself.

Trust yourself. Trust the process. Trust God.

A Final Word on Trust

Trust is not about handing over power. It is about stepping into a rhythm bigger than yourself. It is about releasing fear, loosening the grip, allowing the divine to lead without hesitation. Because true trust—the kind that transforms—requires both surrender and strength. It asks you to lean in, to risk, to let go of the illusion of control. It is not weakness; it is wisdom.

It is knowing that in the hands of the right Partner, you will not fall. You can practice trust in these three important ways:

- Trust yourself to begin.
- Trust the process even when it doesn't make sense.
- Trust God to hold what you can't.

Trust is giving yourself to another, to be weak, to be naked, to be unashamed. It is stepping into divine love that sees your wounds and does not turn away. True love always tells the truth—even if we can't hear it yet.

The Truth?

You are something and somebody. Say it. Out loud. Right now. "I am something and somebody."

Again. "I am something and somebody." Let it sink in. Let it take root. Stop allowing your unhealed wounds to block the truth. Stop sabotaging yourself. Start the journey of healing by allowing the truth of God's love to heal what has been wounded for far too long.

You are beautiful. You are worthy. You are part of something way bigger than you can even imagine. This is not a finale—it's a new beginning. Throw the S.H.I.T. overboard. Now. Before it's too late. Not because this is the end—but because it's the only way to truly begin.

Music for Meditation

"Trust God" by Carmen Calhoun

Epilogue

MEET ME IN THE SUNFLOWER

Meet me in the sunflower.

There's a place I've been walking toward my entire life. I didn't know it had a name. I just knew I was always looking for somewhere I could finally exhale. I thought it might be in a marriage. I thought it might be when I became enough for someone else to stay. I thought it might be behind a locked door, a key I could never quite get. I thought it might be on the altar of performance, religion, or endurance. But no matter how hard I worked, how much I gave, or how little I asked for, I never found it.

Until one day, after walking through the wreckage of my life—the betrayals, the abuse, the shame, the ship that carried my family's pain and my own—I heard the whisper:

Meet me in the sunflower.

I didn't understand. Sunflower? What does a sunflower have to do with survival, betrayal, or heartbreak? How does a field of fragile petals heal a storm like mine? But before I ever heard it…I had to face something first.

I had to admit that I was bankrupt. Bankrupt from years of giving, shrinking, bargaining, and hoping. Bankrupt from performing roles no one asked me to audition for. Bankrupt from carrying not just my pain, but pain that was handed to me before I even knew I was carrying it.

And when I finally surrendered—when I laid all the broken keys, empty promises, and inherited survival strategies at God's feet—the Holy Spirit didn't hand me a quick fix.

Instead, the Spirit took me deeper. Deeper than my marriages. Deeper than the betrayal. Deeper than the wreckage I called my story. I wasn't just cycling through bad choices. I was sailing an old ship, one I didn't even know I had boarded. I was performing, striving, giving, pleasing, appeasing; not realizing that behind every casserole, every massage, every time I twisted it up to earn love, I was trying to heal an ancient wound with temporary tools.

And then I heard it: *Meet me in the sunflower.*

So, I followed.

I followed through the wreckage, not just of my story but of generations before me. Through the broken ship. Through the shattered mirrors of my story. Through the shame, the hurt, the insecurity, the trouble; the S.H.I.T. that I carried like it was my only inheritance.

And then, there it was.

A field. Golden. Endless. A thousand faces lifted toward the sun without shame. And standing there in the dark-seeded center of the largest sunflower, I saw them: the oppressed and the oppressor, the abandoned and the betrayer, the mother who didn't believe me, the father who didn't defend me, the men who took without asking, the little girl who tried to disappear. They were all there. But they weren't arguing. They weren't fighting. They weren't explaining. They were loving.

I stood frozen. How? How could love survive this?

And then the Holy Spirit whispered back through the field: *It survives because the sun still shines and the Son still reigns.* "The light shines in the darkness, and the darkness has not overcome it." (John 1:5, NIV).

And then I heard it again: *Meet me in the sunflower.*

And looking back, I realize it wasn't just Shame, Hurt, Insecurity, and Trouble. It was also the quiet, hidden things— worry, jealousy, anxiety, the constant need for approval, the overthinking. The ship wasn't just wood and chains, it was *me*, tangled in every voice that told me I wasn't enough. This was the place where forgiveness outshined bitterness. Where anger had no more footing. Where healing wasn't about pretending it didn't hurt but about laying it down. Where I saw, for the first time, the ship is not the end of the story.

The field is.

The sunflower is.

The garden of the healed, the reconciled, the free.

The ones who survived the ship, threw their S.H.I.T. overboard, and finally stood in the sunlight to meet God, themselves, and their ancestors in a field where love was stronger than captivity and where the sun always finds you.

I stood there, barefoot and undone. The invitation was still echoing.

Meet me in the sunflower.

Not when you're perfect. Not when you've figured it all out. Not when you've earned it. But now. As you are. With everything you carry. And be filled—to overflow with the love of God—so that you, and others, can be healed.

Music to Celebrate Healing and Unity

"We are One" by Carmen Calhoun

www.ingramcontent.com/pod-product-compliance
Lightning Source LLC
Chambersburg PA
CBHW050443150626
46551CB00028B/1210